D1598307

VOODOO

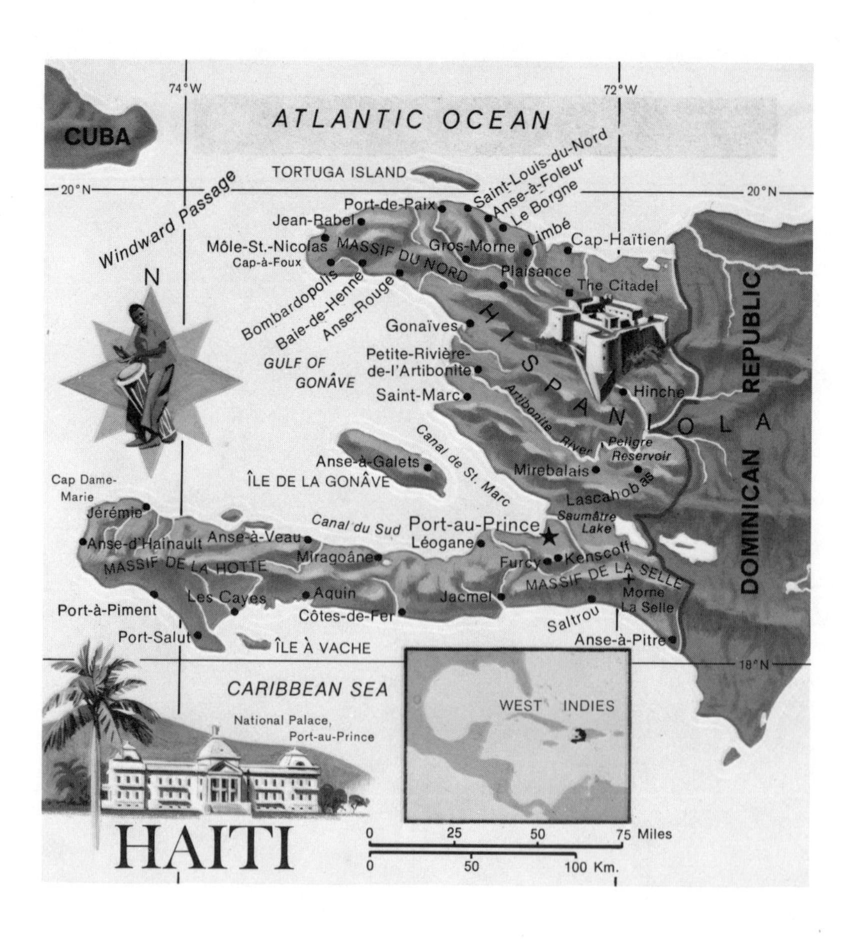

ATLANTIC OCEAN
CUBA
74°W
72°W
20°N
18°N
TORTUGA ISLAND
Windward Passage
Port-de-Paix
Saint-Louis-du-Nord
Anse-à-Foleur
Le Borgne
Jean-Rabel
Môle-St.-Nicolas
Cap-à-Foux
MASSIF DU NORD
Gros-Morne
Limbé
Cap-Haïtien
Plaisance
The Citadel
Bombardopolis
Baie-de-Henne
Anse-Rouge
Gonaïves
HISPANIOLA
GULF OF GONÂVE
Petite-Rivière-de-l'Artibonite
Saint-Marc
Artibonite River
Hinche
Peligre Reservoir
DOMINICAN REPUBLIC
Canal de St. Marc
Anse-à-Galets
ÎLE DE LA GONÂVE
Mirebalais
Lascahobas
Cap Dame-Marie
Jérémie
Canal du Sud
Port-au-Prince
Saumâtre Lake
Anse-d'Hainault
Anse-à-Veau
Léogane
MASSIF DE LA HOTTE
Miragoâne
Furcy
Kenscoff
MASSIF DE LA SELLE
Morne La Selle
Port-à-Piment
Les Cayes
Aquin
Jacmel
Côtes-de-Fer
Saltrou
Port-Salut
ÎLE À VACHE
Anse-à-Pitre
CARIBBEAN SEA
National Palace, Port-au-Prince
WEST INDIES
HAITI
0 25 50 75 Miles
0 50 100 Km.

VOODOO

ITS ORIGINS AND PRACTICES

BY HENRY GILFOND

FRANKLIN WATTS
NEW YORK | LONDON | 1976

Photographs courtesy of:
Hirmer Fotoarchiv: p. 1; New York Public Library Picture Collection: pp. 8, 63; Alan Band Associates: p. 10; Stuart Newman Associates: p. 13; UNESCO: p. 16; United Nations/J. Viesti: p. 17; Reprinted by permission of Schocken Books, Inc., from *Voodoo in Haiti* by Alfred Metraux, © 1959 by Alfred Metraux: pp. 18, 20, 51, 72, 86; André Held Editeur: p. 23; *Isles of Rhythm* by E. Leaf, published by A. S. Barnes & Company, Inc.: pp. 24, 38; The American Museum of Natural History: p. 26; Chelsea House Publishers, New York: pp. 42, 45.

Library of Congress Cataloging in Publication Data

Gilfond, Henry.
Voodoo, its origins and practices.

Bibliography: p.
Includes index.
SUMMARY: Discusses the history, beliefs, and rituals of voodoo, with emphasis on its practice in Haiti.
1. Voodooism—Juvenile literature. [1. Voodooism] I. Title.
BL2490.G54 299′.6 76–16046
ISBN 0–531–00347–7

Printed in the United States of America
6 5 4 3 2

To All The Faithful

CONTENTS

VOODOO

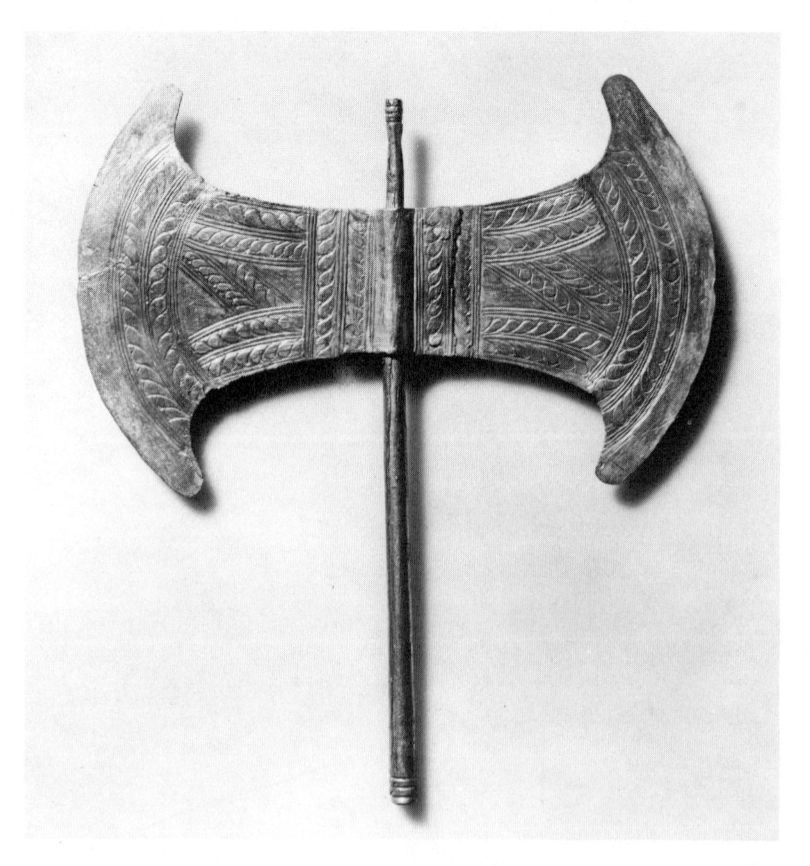

A gold double-ax found in a cave in Crete. Originally it was used to slay sacrificial animals.

1

ROOTS—AFRICAN HERITAGE

The roots of voodoo are African. Africa is a continent of great variety—peoples, animals, plant life, culture. Its religions, too, are varied, each with its own mythology and each with its own system of theology and observance. The notion that African religion is sorcery, witchcraft, and primitive idol worship—the popular idea in the West—served Europeans who exploited Africa and its people. The truth of the matter is that African faiths are immeasurably profound in their beliefs and thoroughly sophisticated in their practice.

As many anthropologists have informed us, Africa has kept alive many tenets and rituals "inherited from the ancient religions of the classical East and of the Aegean world." The double-ax employed in the religious rites of ancient Crete, for example, is still employed in the worship of the African god, Shango. According to the highly respected anthropologist Alfred Metraux, the religion of the people of the Guinea Coast of Africa is so full of sophisticated subtlety that its beliefs and rituals could have been developed only by a highly learned priesthood with plenty of time for theological speculation.

The Africans who were forced into slavery and brought

to the Western Hemisphere, the originators of the voodoo faith, were for the most part from the Guinea Coast, the West African seaboard stretching from the Senegalese River on the north to modern Nigeria's eastern borders. The great majority of them were of the Ashanti, the Fon, and the Yoruba peoples. They had been welded together by a long history of wars and conquests into more or less homogeneous kingdoms. The customs, faiths, and rituals of these peoples had much in common. There were some differences, however, in their religious mythologies, mythologies which have provided us with many clues to the mysteries of voodoo.

African religions may be termed monotheistic, in that each sect believes that there is one supreme god. They may be termed polytheistic, too, inasmuch as each of the African religious orders worships a pantheon of gods. Like religions everywhere, African religions are concerned with creation: the creation of the earth, the skies, the sun, the moon, the stars, the waters and, of course, humans. Each African faith has its own version of this creation.

Nyame is the Ashanti supreme god. He is the sky-god and the rain-god. His wife, Asase Ya, represents the earth. The marriage of "the sky" and "the earth" has produced four children. The four children have given birth to all the hundreds of nature deities, gods of the trees, the stones, and the waters.

Perhaps one of the more unique characters in Ashanti mythology is Ananse, the Spider. It was Ananse who shaped the first humans (to whom Nyame gave life). Ananse is credited with creating the sun, the moon, the stars, and alternating day and night. He is reputedly the first king of the Ashanti and the inventor of grain.

It is Ananse who acts as an intermediary between humans and the supreme god, Nyame. Ananse carries the complaints and the special pleadings of humans on earth to the Ashanti supreme being. The intermediary plays an important role in voodoo. It was as an intermediary that Ananse told Nyame that humans were desperate for rain. Nyame delivered the rain, as the humans asked, but in such quantities that it created a flood reminiscent of the flood of Biblical Noah's time. Nyame sent a hot wind to dry up the mess, then made a hurried retreat to his abode in the skies, so he wouldn't have to be bothered any more by people.

Interesting, too, from the viewpoint of comparative religious studies, is the Ashanti story of their river-god, Tano. Tano, according to the legend, deprived his older brother of his heritage by practicing a deception on their blind father. In the Bible, it was by deceiving his father (whose eyes had grown dim) that Jacob deprived his older brother Esau of his rightful inheritance.

The Yoruba have other names for their sky-god and their earth-goddess, Olorun (or Obtala) and Odudua. From their union and the union of their children came all the nature deities, such as Shango the rain-god, Oshun the river-goddess, and Ogun the iron-god. These names, in one form or another, will appear again in the study of the voodoo gods.

The Fon were a warlike people and absorbed all the gods of the peoples they conquered into their own pantheon. As a consequence, they have several different names for their supreme being: Mahu, Nana Buluku, and Se. For some among the Fon, Mahu is the principal god. For most, however, Mahu and Lisa, the twin children of Nana Buluku, are supreme.

Lisa is representative of the male forces: the sky, the sun, power. Mahu is representative of the female forces: the earth, the moon, fertility. Together they gave birth to a son, Dan, also a twin, who is representative of the motion of life on the earth and in the universe. Dan also represents the unity in the world, the balance between the earth and the sky, night and day, work and rest. According to the Fon people, Dan is life and Mahu is thought. The twin concept, so important to the Fon, tends to explain the elements and forces in life which are simultaneously contradictory and complementary. (The twin concept is important in voodoo as well.)

Dan, like all gods, can take any number of shapes and forms. Perhaps the most important of those forms is the rainbow circling the earth. It is in the shape of the rainbow that Dan is known as Dan Ayido Hwedo. In the figures and drawings created in his worship, Dan is represented as a snake biting its own tail. (The snake, we will discover, is a most important figure and symbol in voodoo rites and worship.)

Dan is also responsible for the control of all the activities and actions of the numerous nature gods in the Fon pantheon. In the Fon language the word for nature god is Vodu, from which the word "voodoo" perhaps was born. There are several major groups of Vodu in the Fon lists of gods: the sky-gods, the thunder-gods, the earth gods, and the fate-gods. There are also the ancestor-gods and Legba, servant to the gods and intermediary between humans and their deities. (It is Legba who became perhaps the most important deity in the pantheon which was to develop in voodoo.)

Time and distance, and the hardships of slavery, helped develop many differences between the beliefs and religious practices of the Africans in their homeland and the practices of African slaves abroad. Yet much remained and remains related, if not identical. The voodoo gods, Damballa-Wedo, Aida-Wedo, Hevioso, Agassu, Erzilie, Ogun,

Shango, and many others, are still worshiped in Africa. Music and dance are essential to voodoo as well as African ritual. The sacrifice of animals, usually domestic, or fowl (an ancient tradition and probably a substitute for the more ancient tradition of human sacrifice) is a religious rite practiced in Africa as well as in voodoo. The ritual usages of the blood of the sacrifice, and the eating of its flesh are seen in both. Perhaps the most dramatic of religious experiences in voodoo is the phenomenon of "possession," those moments when a god enters the head of one of the faithful and the worshiper becomes the god in spirit, in action, and in speech. This phenomenon is as integral to African practices as it is to voodoo rites in the Western Hemisphere.

Many peoples from many different areas of western Africa contributed to the fashioning of voodoo in the Western world. We shall explore the contributions of Christianity and European folklore in later chapters. But, unquestionably, the Yoruba and especially the Fon were the greatest influence in structuring voodoo as it evolved in the New World. Voodoo, as we said earlier, comes from the Fon word Vodu. *Hungan,* as the voodoo priest is called, means "master of the god" in Fon. The sacred pitchers used in voodoo ritual are called "govi," the sacred pot is called "zin," the sacred rattle "asson." Today these are the names of these sacred objects in Dahomey, the African homeland of the Fon.

Alfred Metraux said of voodoo that it is often little more than an impoverished example of the religious systems to be found on the Guinea Coast of Africa. Still, for its faithful, voodoo is a rich and forceful factor in their lives. Nor can they forget that this voodoo, at least in the black Republic of Haiti, served them well, even heroically, in their struggle for freedom.

2

VOODOO—THE BEGINNING

There is no exact count of the slaves brought out of Africa and shipped to the New World. The estimates are enormous. Some historians say that at least 900,000 (some say more than 2 million) were taken from the Guinea Coast for the French West Indian island of Saint Domingue (now Haiti and the Dominican Republic).

A man, a woman, may be forcibly removed from their homeland, from familiar surroundings and faces, but the memory of places, the memory of those they cherished, the memory of freedom cannot be erased even by the brutality of slavery. The Africans arrived in the New World in chains, but their minds were free, their thoughts were free, and their faith in their gods, though tried, was as yet undiminished.

The nature of the African slaves' gods changed with time, mirroring the abject poverty and the humility their worshipers suffered. The gods lost some of their heroic stature, became humbler in their dress and manner. The rites too lost some of their glamour, became simpler, even impoverished. Slaves did not have the means or the time for sumptuous ceremony.

Although changed, the gods survived. In Portuguese

Brazil, African faith and practice survived as Macumba, a faith which even today increases in adherents and strength. In Jamaica, the faith brought from Africa continues to flourish as Obeah. In Trinidad it is Shango. In Cuba it was the Lucumi (or Yoruba) religions which persisted, and today—though strongly influenced by Catholic ritual—Santeria flourishes. In the United States, around New Orleans and the Carolinas, African worship continued. African worship went on in Colombia, Venezuela, and for a time in Argentina; in short, everywhere the Africans were forced to labor in slavery. It was in Haiti, however, that the faith the Africans brought from their continent persisted and developed most significantly.

The slave owners, from the very beginning, feared any sign of African worship. The owners saw to it that slaves who spoke the same language were separated. For any communication among slaves had potential for riot and rebellion. The greatest of common ties among the slaves was their faith in and their worship of African gods, and the slave owners made every effort to prevent such worship. Slaves suspected of practicing voodoo were whipped, tortured, even branded.

In 1664, the lieutenant general of the French West Indies Islands, a M. de Tracy, issued a decree which ordered all slave owners to have their slaves baptized Catholic and to instruct them in the "Catholic, Apostolic and Roman religion." Similar decrees were issued by the other colonial powers in the New World. Undoubtedly there were some among the Christian clergymen who thought that by following the decree they were doing God's work: bringing lost souls into the Church. But, saving lost souls was not the purpose of the decrees.

The 1664 decree was followed by the Code Noir (Black Code) in March of 1685. The Code strengthened the ini-

Slaves working on a sugar cane plantation

tial decree by imposing fines on any slave holder who failed to baptize his slaves as ordered. It went further in its attack on African worship. It prohibited any kind of meeting or assembly of the slaves except for the purpose of Catholic worship, and threatened fines and other punishments for the slave owners who were lax in carrying out this mandate.

In Haiti, the initial order to baptize the slaves was carried out without incident. The slaves were familiar with baptism. It was an ancient African ritual as well. The slaves considered baptism by the Church as perhaps just another magical rite and they looked upon the unbaptized slaves as inferiors. There was very little instruction in the "Catholic, Apostolic and Roman religion," because slave owners believed that Church instruction might prove dangerous. After all, the Church *did* preach a certain kind of equality among people.

When some Jesuit priests took seriously their mission of spreading the teachings of the Church, slave owners saw to it that they were expelled from the colonies. The slave owners even opposed, if perhaps not vigorously, the celebration of Christian holy days. Such celebrations took the slaves out of the fields thereby diminishing their production and the owner's profits.

Actually, the slave owners did not have to concern themselves too much with Church instruction. In general, the priests who were shipped to the slave colonies were of a rather poor quality. What did concern the slave owners was the nighttime sound of the drums from the distant hills. The concern was well-founded. The drums were African, the drummers were escaped slaves.

Saint Domingue, in those early years, was the richest colony in the Western Hemisphere. It was known as the "Pearl of the Antilles" because of the wealth it brought its French slave owners. But to the blacks from Africa, the producers of that wealth, it gave nothing but back-breaking, life-sapping labor and an early death. Slaves were worked in the sugar fields in Saint Domingue (and we will stay in Saint Domingue, for it is here that voodoo was born) from sunrise until ten and eleven o'clock in the evening. Some modern-day Haitian historians maintain the field slave's life span was as brief as two or three years. Other authorities say ten years.

A Nigerian voodoo priest at a shrine to Ogun

Still, in the blackness of the night, for all the aching in their arms and legs, for all their weariness, slaves listened for the drums in the hills and, in the darkness, secretly chanted and danced African religious rituals, as they were remembered. Some managed to steal away to join other runaways. These escaped slaves were called Maroons, a corruption of the French word *marron,* the Spanish word *cimarron,* meaning "wild," "untamed." The Maroons were the most instrumental in keeping alive the memory of African gods and ritual, and in fashioning the Haitian pantheon of voodoo gods.

The voodoo that developed on Saint Domingue was actually an amalgam of faiths. According to Moreau de Saint-Méry, a French writer of the late eighteenth century, there were Wolofs, Bambara, Ararads, Minas, Fon, Mondongues, Nago, Mahi, and many other African people working the sugar plantations. This would indicate that slaves from almost every part of western Africa lived on the island, something more modern anthropologists are likely to doubt. However, if there were only slaves from the African Gold Coast in Saint Domingue, there would still be, as already described, any number of religious mythologies, pantheons of gods, and different religious rituals among the slaves. The difference in gods, rites, and ceremonies, however, were considerably less significant than their similarities. Each people believed in a supreme god and a pantheon of nature gods, intermediaries, and ancestor gods. Their rituals followed similar patterns. There were the singing of sacred chants, the beating of sacred drums and other instruments, dancing, and "possession" by the gods.

How did the amalgamation of faiths work? Most often the voodoo that developed bore the mark of the most powerful group in a particular area. Where the Ibo people were more numerous, the Ibo traditions would predominate. Where the Mandingos were more numerous, as in the north of Haiti, it was their traditions which were more likely to be followed. In the south of the island it was the Arada people who were predominant. There were other people and, later, still more with different practices.

By edict, all the slaves on Saint Domingue had been baptized. Nominally they were Catholics. They learned to speak their Paternosters and their Ave Marias. Yet, the Catholic Church was never powerful enough to wipe out the worship of African gods. Quite the opposite, in time voodoo absorbed what it wanted from Christian practice.

For the followers of voodoo, the Christian God was too far away, somewhere up in the sky, and much too busy to attend to the needs and wishes of the ordinary people down on earth. So when voodoo followers needed help, they called on their *loa.* In Haiti these were nature gods that the common man and woman could approach. They could be invoked to join the assemblies, they could hear, be heard, and even touched. The loa would remain at the center of the black Haitian's voodoo faith.

Voodoo Rebels

The first recorded slave insurrection on Saint Domingue occurred in 1522, nineteen years after the first West Africans were landed on the island in 1503. It was a brief rebellion, however, as were the others of 1533, 1537, 1548, 1679, 1704, and those in years that followed. There were too many obstacles in the way of organizing a successful rebellion. There was scarcely any communication between plantations and on each plantation little talk among the slaves was allowed. There was also the extreme vigilance of the white owners. They were constantly alert to the possibility of slave rebellion, and particularly wary of the evidence of voodoo among their slaves. Voodoo, they recognized correctly, was the one element in the life of the slaves which united them.

Early in the life of the colony, the French colonial administrators, in their reports back to France, described voodoo as the road to slave rebellion. Voodoo, they wrote, could prove "a terrible weapon" against the French control of the island. Voodoo, they cautioned, puts the French administration of Saint Domingue "under a constant threat of assault."

A procession of leaders rose up to lead the slaves on

The Citadel, a fortress near Haiti's north coast built by King Henri Christophe

Saint Domingue to freedom—Macandal, Romaine Riviere, Jean-Francois, Biassou, Hyacinthe Ducoudray, Halou, Boukman, Vincent Ogé, and finally Toussaint Louverture —under whose assaults the French were severely weakened —and Jacques Dessalines and Henri Christophe, who drove out the French for good. The liberated part of the island was named Haiti. The other part where slavery continued was called Santo Domingo.

Except for the opposition of the Catholic Church, nothing stopped voodoo from becoming a powerful religion on the island. With the ascendancy in 1849 of Soulouque, who named himself Faustin I, "Emperor of All the People," voodoo practices—drum, dance and sacrifice—came openly to the palace, for the emperor and his wife, Empress Adelina, were faithful adherents to voodoo.

3

VOODOO GODS

At the center of voodoo worship are the *loa,* a word generally translated to mean "god" or "gods." Actually, loa is a Congolese word meaning "spirit," and the voodoo loa are also considered spirits. They make up voodoo's pantheon of nature gods, and may be saints or angels or even demons. They are the deities who control the well-being, the fortune and the fate of the voodoo faithful. Loa are always near at hand, and they can do good or create mischief.

Gods in every culture tend to reflect those who create them. We may be better able to understand the voodoo deities, the shapes they take, their attitudes, their manners, their needs and desires, their functions, if we know something more of the lives of those who worship them.

In the days of slavery, when voodoo had just begun to take shape, the slaves were housed in something like an open corral. They lived in huts with walls made of wattled twigs and daub. They had little if any furniture and their tables were mats of straw.

The law of the land required that the slave master provide his slaves with a set minimum food ration. But except for the laws against the congregating of the slaves, the owners ignored government regulations concerning the care and treatment of slaves. They gave their slaves just enough rice or oatmeal, crackers, herring and molasses to keep them alive. The law said slaves were to be given two cotton garments each year. But this law too was ignored, and often, slaves wore nothing at all.

Whippings and beatings were administered without mercy and often for the most trivial reasons. Slave men suffered most, but women were not exempt from such cruelties. Nor were the more favored house-slaves immune to the brutality of the slave owners. A slave-cook who spoiled a dessert might be thrown alive into an oven. Faine Scharon, in a history of Toussaint Louverture and the revolution in Saint Domingue, wrote of white women who had women servant-slaves killed because they were suspected of intimacies with their white owners.

It is not surprising that the slaves began to see their gods as less than the magnificent and heroic protectors that they were in Africa. The abject poverty of slave life, the humility of servitude, the degradations suffered at every moment would not be allowed by gods who were mighty and powerful. We shall see, as we begin to examine the loa and compare some of them to their African antecedents, that the life of the slaves changed the nature, if not the substance of African gods.

The Loa

Legba is perhaps the most important loa in the voodoo faith. In Africa, among the Fon people, Legba is the interpreter of the will of the gods. He is always the first of the gods in the Fon pantheon to be honored in religious rites.

The great majority of Haiti's urban dwellers and rural peasants are poor.

He is responsible for delivering the messages of the gods to earth. He is the god of destiny. A wood or iron fetish honors him in every Fon household.

In Haiti, Legba has become a limping old man dressed in rags. This reflects the African's profound loss of dignity. In his role as Legba Pié Cassé (in voodoo as well as in the Fon pantheon, the gods take many roles) his legs are paralyzed, his arms stiff and crooked. As Legba Avarda, he is a tramp, hobo, a vagabond. Sometimes he is just an old man who walks unsteadily with the help of a cane. He has lost the majestic bearing he carries among the Fon. Still, in voodoo, it is Legba who must be honored first in any ceremonial ritual. It is he who opens the barriers at

the rites, permitting the appearance of all the other gods of the voodoo pantheon. He is the guardian of the doors of every house. He is also the guardian of all the highways, the paths and the crossroads, and this last gives him a significance his Fon counterpart does not possess. It is at the crossroads that much of the work of the voodoo magicians is initiated and performed, and it is Legba, taking the form of Legba-Carrefour, who is the chief loa at all the ceremonies pertaining to voodoo magic.

Legba lives at the crossroads, of streets, lanes, highways. (Each of the loa in voodoo has a special dwelling place, or places.) Reflecting the appetites of the Haitian people, if not their larders, he likes to eat lots of meat and to drink

The voodoo symbol for the loa Damballa

rum and other alcoholic beverages. Legba has other very human characteristics. For example, he is particular about his clothing. He likes his clothes to be black or yellow.

It must be noted that the loa may differ from one place to another. Their characteristics, clothes, food and drink may change within an area as small as a few blocks.

It should be noted, too, for the sake of clarity, that the loa, or "mystère," as they are also called, do not appear in flesh and blood at the voodoo rituals. The loa are spirits. They are invoked by the drums and chants of the faithful, and make their presence known by possessing a worshiper. In possession, the loa enters the person's head. The worshiper who has been taken over will take on all of that loa's personal characteristics—dress, speech, and actions. At such moments the loa is said to be "riding his horse." We shall explore possession when we come to the investigation of the voodoo rituals. Right now, let us stay with the more significant of the voodoo loa and see how the Haitian pantheon of loa grew.

Damballa is another of the Haitian loa who suffered much in his transition from Africa. Damballa is one of the manifestations of the Fon god Dan, whose great significance in the Fon theology has already been indicated. As the rainbow, he is a spiral around the earth and holds it together. He moves the sun, the moon and the stars. He separates the waters and creates mountains. In Haiti, he is the snake god. The French historian, Moreau de Saint-Méry, wrote that he witnessed a ritual in which a live snake was used, but this was in the 1700s and long before voodoo took its present form.

The snake still has a role in voodoo ritual, but only as a symbol. Damballa is not a snake; he is a snake god. He is a strong god, as he was in Africa, but there the similarities end. In Haiti Damballa is ugly. He drinks too

The voodoo symbol for the loa Erzilie

much. He gets drunk too often. He is given to rolling around in a drunken stupor. Because of his strength he is to be avoided at the voodoo ceremonies if one is to escape bodily harm. Damballa is not without redeeming qualities. He is reputed to be able to cure certain severe illnesses, and his favor is often sought for this reason. But he is a jealous god and the voodoo faithful must take care not to arouse his jealousy lest he deliver some dreadful evil on them.

Ogun, the protective god of war, has kept much of his African dignity. As Ogun Badagi, he endows his followers with the gift of prophecy. As Ogun Batal, he transmits an ability to cure ailments. As Ogun Balandjo, he watches over those who travel, keeping them safe from accident and harm. As Ogun, he protects his worshipers from the wounds of bullets, knives, machetes, and other weapons. His favorite color is red, and it was his color that the soldiers who fought for the liberation of Haiti wore on their sleeves in battle.

The most charming of the loa in the voodoo pantheon is Erzilie. More than all others, she most probably mirrors the dreams of opulence which must come occasionally to the miserably poor of Haiti. Erzilie is beautiful, elegant, and enormously wealthy. Her clothing is made of the richest silks and other fine cloths. Sometimes they are brilliantly colored, sometimes of the purest white. She also wears the finest jewelry—beautiful gold rings and gold necklaces.

Erzilie is gentle, kind and sensitive. She does not like bad people. To the good, she brings help, good will and good fortune. Mirroring a lightness of life for which the Haitians must yearn, Erzilie is something of a flirt. For all the whimsy this might involve, however, Erzilie always behaves like a queen. It was as a queen that she is reputed to have fought in the ranks of the inspired armies which battled for Haiti's independence.

Gede, or Guede, is one of the two loa most associated with death. It is Gede to whom the "bocors" (practitioners of black magic) turn when they want somebody murdered. It is the loa Gede who digs the graves for victims of black magic—as well as for those who die of natural causes or by accident.

He makes his appearance at the voodoo rituals wearing a high hat and a black robe and carrying a knife. He looks like a dead man whose burial is long overdue. He is an unpleasant loa, as might be expected. His speech is harsh, he talks through his nose, and he is garrulous. He goes about at the ritual beating all those who are "possessed" by other gods.

Gede generally lives in the cemeteries behind a cross, but he is also known to make his home in cities, at a village crossroads, or on a rural thoroughfare. Wherever he is, the evil magicians come to consult with him about their evil enterprises. He likes to eat fried plantains and fish, but he especially enjoys black chicken. He avoids alcoholic beverages and his favorite color is black.

Baron Samedi is the other of the loa associated with death. He is the dwarf who comes with clanking chains to the voodoo rituals. Like Gede, he lives behind a cross in the cemeteries. Like Gede, he is very much feared.

The bocor must speak with Baron Samedi before he can create a "wanga," an evil charm, to kill someone. The bocor needs Baron Samedi's approval, or else the evil charm will not work. Gede too must approve of the bocor's intentions. Gede is the final judge in such situations and he is believed to be just. If Gede does not consider the intended murder to be justified, he will refuse to dig the grave for the proposed victim. Without a prepared grave, according to voodoo belief, there can be no murder.

Baron Samedi never disputes Gede's decisions. He is a busy loa, and one corpse more or less does not matter to him. Sometimes, however, when there is a disagreement between the two loa, there will be some sort of compromise.

A painting of Baron Samedi by Haitian artist Préfète Duffaut

The bocor's evil wanga may cause the victim to develop a grave illness but he will not die.

The Saints

The voodoo pantheon contains loa which originated in the Catholic Church. Some say that a person who is not a

A household voodoo altar with lithographs of Christian saints

good Catholic cannot be a good voodooist. Voodoo Catholics believe with all other Catholics, that God, the Creator, is the ruler of the universe. They send their prayers to God, to Jesus, Mary, the Holy Spirit, and they venerate the saints. They accept the belief that God has granted each person a soul and that after death the soul returns to God to be eternally rewarded or punished. (In voodoo a person has two souls, a fact that we will discuss later.) For the voodooist, God is too far away in the heavens to pay any attention to the ordinary lives of people on earth. So, too, are Jesus and Mary. The saints are something else again.

By far the largest number of the voodoo faith, who are also practicing Catholics, simply regard all saints as loa, though they understand that all loa are not saints. Saint Patrick, for example, has become identical with (or a manifestation of) the voodoo snake god, Damballa. Saint Anthony is identified with Legba. The Virgin Mary, Mater Dolorosa, is the gentle, queenly, beautiful Erzilie. Saint Peter, Saint Paul, Saint Francis and numberless other saints have their counterparts among the loa.

Others of the voodoo faith have developed a more complicated method of moving the saints into their pantheon. They believe that for each saint in heaven there is a corresponding loa who lives under the waters. These loa rise regularly to meet with the saints somewhere between heaven and earth. At these meetings the loa relay the wishes and prayers of people to the saints. The saints then return to God with these messages. God, who is never too busy to listen to the saints, then grants or denies whatever petition has been made by His mortals.

A third, and by far the smallest group of the faithful, has a sharply different view of the relationship between loa and saint. They believe that at one time all loa were the angels of God, but that they had fallen from his grace. They believe, too, that the saints and loa are eternal and bitter enemies.

There are many other loa in the voodoo pantheon: Agaou, Shango, Congo, Cibi, Simalo and more. Every voodoo priest has his or her own list of loa. Every family has its own personal loa. The pantheon of these lesser voodoo gods is in a continuous state of expansion. The loa themselves are continuously assuming other manifestations, other names, and other characteristics. This is a process that takes place in every region, city, and hamlet of Haiti, and even in the temples of each individual priest. In addition, the great and most honored of the voodoo priests become loa. So do some of the Haitian folk heroes or national heroes. Dead family members can become loa

An Ibeji, a West African fetish figure. When a twin dies, the surviving twin keeps an Ibeji to appease the spirit of the dead brother or sister.

too. The souls of the dead are of critical importance in voodoo worship and in the daily lives of voodoo believers. We shall explore this aspect in a later chapter.

Marassa

Among the rituals and practices of voodoo, one which must especially puzzle the Western mind is the worship of the *marassa,* the voodoo word for twins. For some, the marassa are as supernaturally powerful as the loa. For others, they are even more powerful. Twins who are alive are approached as if they were living loa. Twins who have died are worshiped as gods.

If one digs deep into anthropological studies, one can find other, mostly primitive, cultures in which twins have magical powers—for good or evil. Some African societies believed twins were a great danger and put them and their mother to death. In Central Africa, among certain peoples, the mother and father of twins are thought to have the power to increase the fruit of their plantain trees. On the other hand, the father of twins among certain peoples in Uganda is put into a state of taboo. He is forbidden to kill anything. He is not even permitted to look at blood.

The Nutka Indian tribe of British Columbia believe that twins are endowed with the power to make rain, or change the weather. So do the Tsimshian, the Thompson and Shushwap Indians.

Indians of Peru believe twins are the children of lightning and can make rain.

In the central areas of India, Hindus bury their dead twins near a lake to keep them moist. They believe that pouring water on their graves will bring rain.

In Africa, among the Bantu-speaking Baronga people, the mother of twins is called Tilo—the Bantu word for the sky—and it is she who has the power to bring rain.

Evidence of the adoration of twins in the West is found in Greek mythology. Twin sons of the Greek god Zeus became the two stars we call Gemini. It is these Greek twins who, according to legend, have the power to allay storms.

The marassa too, can bring the rains down, if they wish. But they are endowed with other powers as well, particularly the power to create mischief. They can bring illness and hurt to anyone who may vex or displease them. Even ancestral twins, according to voodoo belief, possess these powers.

The marassa are identified with Saint Cosmas and Saint Damian, the legendary twin physicians who were martyred by the Roman emperor, Diocletian. But it is to Saint Nicholas that the voodoo faithful turn for release from the torments the twins visit on them. Saint Nicholas is presumed to be the spiritual father of the marassa. Saint Claire is looked upon as their spiritual mother.

Even more powerful than the marassa, among the faithful, is the dosu (dosa if it is a girl). This is the child born following the birth of the twins. This child is believed to have power equal to that of the marassa siblings. The dosu is treated with even more respect, awe, and perhaps fear, than are the twins.

Marassa are likely to be capricious. They take offense easily, and this is especially hard on the families. A mother dares not scold the marassa, lest one or both visit some evil on her. Similarly, a father must not neglect the wants of his twins. Care must be taken, too, to avoid antagonism between the marassa. It is believed that the twins hate each other even before they are born and that the antagonism does not diminish at any time in their lives. It is for this reason that their parents are careful to show no preference between them. They are dressed alike, fed alike, and always accorded equal treatment.

It is said that even death does not separate them. If one should die, the other puts something of his food away for his twin brother or sister. They are presumed to share but one soul.

Christmas Day on the voodoo calendar is the day for sacrifices to the twins, both living and dead. As with other voodoo ceremonies, fowl and animals are sacrificed, but vegetables of any kind are forbidden. Vegetables, it is believed, lessen the powers of marassa. There are other taboos, depending on the likes and dislikes of the twins. They will not, for example, eat with knives and forks and spoons. Some will not eat from mats. Others will not eat food placed on banana leaves. They are also jealous, and care must be taken that one is not served before the other. At any ceremony the marassa must eat first. Others may eat only after the twins have had their fill.

Marassa do not often possess a celebrant at a voodoo ritual. But, when this does happen, the possessed becomes a child again. The celebrant will be mean, will be easily angered, will be jealous. Rarely will the possessed person be pleasant and gay. The celebrant will speak with the voice of the child and will make childish demands. The possessed person is likely to cry when crossed or denied something, but will cringe and plead for mercy if there is any threat of punishment for bad behavior. The possessed celebrant will happily demonstrate how much he knows in reading or arithmetic or some other school subject.

Some consider the marassa God's first children. Some say the twins are the parents of all the loa, and in a number of areas it is not Legba, but the marassa who are the first of the spirits addressed in voodoo ritual. Together with the dosu (or dosa) they are sometimes deemed a sacred trinity, much like the Holy Trinity of the Catholic Church. Others believe that the marassa are not affected by the laws of nature, because of their divinity. And there are those among the voodoo faithful who believe all of these conjectures.

Whatever the case, the marassa constitute an element in faith which is certainly unique to voodoo. Alive or dead, the twins are a mystic and powerful force in the lives of those who worship the voodoo gods, spirits, saints, and deities.

The Voodoo Dead

The voodoo dead rank third, behind the loa and marassa, in importance to voodoo life. There is much of the religious in the voodoo ceremonies for the dead. There is much more which is magic.

Dessunin is the voodoo term for the separation of the soul from the body. According to voodoo belief, a person has two souls. There is the "gros-bon-ange" or personal soul and there is the loa "mait-tete." This is the loa that enters a person the first time he or she is possessed. After the first possession the loa mait-tete and the person are joined together for life. Only death can separate them. The mait-tete loa will return to its home in the waters which flow deep under the earth, once it is separated from its corpse. The children of the dead person inherit his or her loa mait-tete, and it may come back to possess them. The gros-bon-ange goes down to the waters, too, but it is not expected to return to the dead person's children. It will lie in the waters for a year and a day, then in another voodoo ceremony, it will be put to rest permanently.

The hungan (voodoo priest) conducting the ritual for the dead begins, as he usually begins each voodoo rite, with an appeal to the loa to attend his congregation. This more or less formal opening is immediately followed by perhaps the most dramatic, certainly the most eerie, of all voodoo rituals. The hungan lifts the sheet which covers the corpse, moves under the sheet and lies over the body of the dead person. His face on the corpse, he shakes his sacred rattle and again calls on the loa to join the rites. He speaks into the ear of the deceased in whispers, then loudly calls the dead person's name. At this the corpse rises, then falls back on its bed.

It may be, as some observers have reported, that the hungan lifts the body with his hands. To voodoo believers, however, the body moves because the loa is leaving it. In voodoo, it is essential that the loa leave the body of the dead. If it should remain with the corpse, the family of the dead person will be plagued with ill health and other misfortunes.

There are other voodoo precautions deemed necessary by the hungan. He draws the sign of the cross in flour on the forehead of the corpse. He passes feathers plucked from a chicken over its head. He takes the feathers and nail parings of the dead person's left hand and left foot and puts them into a govi (pot). The pot, symbolically, contains the dead person's gros-bon-ange. The pot is placed in some secure spot for some further ritual, at another time. To possess some part of a person, the voodoo faithful believe, is to possess some power over that individual. What is most feared among these followers of the voodoo faith is that such power may be used for an evil purpose, to hurt, to maim, even to kill. So the nail parings or clipping of hair must be secured against any possibility of falling into the hands of an evil magician, the bocor.

Preparing the body of the deceased is an elaborate ritual. For the voodoo adherent every element of that ritual is heavy with significance and magic.

To prepare the body, a trough is dug in the ground and the corpse is placed into it, to be washed with soap and water sweetened with herbs and leaves, then dried. The nose and ears of the corpse are plugged with cotton wool. Its mouth is kept closed by some kind of cord which is knotted at the top of the head. The cotton wool is to prevent the deceased from hearing anything which might disturb him in his grave, and to prevent him from saying anything which might bring harm to his family. His big toes are tied together to make it difficult for him to rise from his grave and walk.

The corpse is dressed in a black suit. The pockets are slashed and turned inside out to make certain the dead carries nothing to the cemetery which might be used against the living.

Anything which was attached to the person before he died must be destroyed or buried. Even the water which was used to wash the dead is generally poured into a deep hole. All those who have touched the corpse in the burial rites must cleanse their hands with specially prepared leaves and water.

In voodoo, each person is said to carry three drops of moisture with him throughout his life and even to his resting place. This is the only reminder of life the departed is permitted. And here, too, meticulous care must be taken, lest these three drops of moisture fall into the hands of a magician. For this moisture is believed to be very powerful.

Sometimes, before the corpse is placed into its coffin, its head and the rest of its body will be shaved clean and all of its fingernails and toenails pared. The hair and the nail parings are placed in the coffin along with a comb, a handkerchief and a rosary. The dead are never buried with shoes, lest they make too much noise in their comings and goings. Nor is any money buried with them, lest they return to take whatever money the family has kept for itself. Pins and needles, too, must be kept out of the coffin for fear of the harm the dead might inflict with them on the living.

Once the voodoo preparations for burial are completed, the local priest in the larger communities, the bush priest (not ordained by the Church) in the rural areas, is called in to read the prayers of the Church and to lead in the singing of the Church canticles. This done, the relatives and guests, one by one, approach the coffin to speak to the deceased. What they have to say to the dead is not in the form of a farewell address, but rather in the form of a message, or a special request. They will ask the corpse to deliver their greetings to someone who is already dead. Or they will ask it to plead for some good fortune with the spirit of someone departed.

The wake takes place in the evening. The voodoo wake is essentially similar to wakes the world over. There are flowers on a table, images of saints, a crucifix, some lighted candles and perhaps an oil lamp. There is food and drink for the relatives and guests. There are occasional outbursts of grief and weeping. There is more chanting and singing of hymns, particularly Church hymns.

There are aspects of the wake that are not usually part of Christian ritual. The family and guests try to amuse the dead person and keep him in a good mood. This is usually done by playing amusing card games. When drinks are offered to the guests, they pour a little of the liquid onto the ground. The libation is, presumably, for the voodoo trinity—the loa, the marassa, and the dead.

The wake comes to an end before the sun rises. The

corpse must be moved out of the house before daybreak. Should the funeral procession begin in sunlight, another member of the family would be sure to die.

A priest, or a bush priest, leads the procession out of the house of mourning. Beyond the threshold, he blesses the corpse, speaks the Catholic prayers, chants some verses of Catholic canticle, then heads the procession toward the cemetery.

With most faiths, the funeral procession travels at a slow pace and takes the most direct route to the cemetery. The voodoo procession, on the other hand, moves swiftly. Sometimes the voodoo cortege will actually begin to run. The route is not direct. The cortege goes down one path, then moves back along another. It will act like a person trying to escape someone who follows. The purpose is to so confuse the corpse that it will not be able to find its way home. Even in the lowering of the body into the grave, the coffin is turned around one last time, to confuse the corpse. Despite these precautions the family will continue to live with the fear that the dead person might return to create mischief.

Fear of the dead rising is touched with something of the religious element in voodoo. It is the magic involved, however, which concerns the voodoo faithful more. Their greatest fear is that the body of the deceased will return without its soul.

Evil magicians are said to raise the dead for evil purposes. Sometimes, to thwart the intentions of a bocor, a plant with many seeds is placed into the coffin with the deceased—the more seeds the better. According to magical prescriptions, the bocor must count all the seeds before he can raise the corpse from its grave. And the count must be completed before sunrise. If the bocor cannot complete the count, the corpse will remain in its coffin.

Following the burial, which has been conducted primarily under the direction of the priest or the bush priest, there is the purely Catholic ritual of the novena, a nine-day devotion dedicated to the departed member of the family. On the first eight days, for a period of some two hours each day, relatives, friends and neighbors assemble in the house of the deceased to hear the priest or bush priest intone the Catholic prayers and to join in the singing of Catholic canticles. An altar has been made of a table and placed in one corner of the room. The table has been covered with a white cloth with colored lithographs of the saints pinned to it. Flowers, a crucifix and candles decorate the altar. Plates of food offerings for the dead have been set on the floor. There is no eating or drinking among the guests.

On the ninth day of the novena, there are a number of changes both in the decor of the room and in the ritual. The walls, windows, and sometimes even the ceiling, are covered with white sheets or curtains. Wreaths are placed on the table altar. More colored lithographs of the saints are attached to the altar. And there is food and drink. Towards midnight, there is the singing of the "libera," a chant to send the dead out of the house. Sometimes it is sung at the cemetery when a permanent cross is erected to mark the grave-site.

The ceremonies which remain to be celebrated for the deceased move further and further away from Church practice. The *mangé mort* (the feeding of the dead) is a ritual sacrifice to all the family ancestors. Food is cooked without salt, then placed in two containers on the table or at its feet. The bush priest blesses the table, blesses the food, sprinkles holy water on both, then leads the gathering out of the room. The door is closed. Outside the door the bush priest leads the family in prayers and in singing Church canticles. Inside the room, the dead are presumed to be feasting on the sacrifice offered them.

After a while, the bush priest knocks at the door three times, then enters to bring out one of the containers of food. One container is for the children and guests of the family. The children scramble, even fight for the food. The second container is generally taken to some crossroad and left there. Presumably the dogs and cats will have a feast.

The last ritual for the dead involves bringing the gros-bon-ange out of the waters. This ritual should be performed one year and one day after the corpse has been buried, but, because of its high cost, it is usually postponed till a number of families can combine their money to pay for the ceremonies.

These rites, as most other voodoo rites, are conducted by a hungan or a mambo (voodoo priestess) at her place of worship, called a humfort. Here the hunsi (assistants), the drums and other musical instruments are assembled and the different families gather under the peristyle. Outside the house of worship, the mambo has erected a tent for herself. The sides are simple white sheets. An oil lamp, burning within the tent, will throw her shadow on the sheets so that her audience will be able to witness the rites she will perform.

Legba, who opens the gates for all the other gods, is invoked. The la-place (the leader of parades at voodoo rites and the master of ceremonies) leads the procession of hunsi —each dressed in white and carrying a govi for the deceased of each family present at the ritual. The hunsi march into the peristyle. They step carefully on mats which have been laid down for them facing the tent. The govi have been decorated with voodoo symbols. The mats lie on the verver, mystic ritual designs drawn by the mambo. The drums, which signaled for the beginning of the procession, continue to beat. The govi are placed in the tent where the mambo sits over a trough of water. The gros-bon-ange of each of the deceased will travel through this water to find its final resting place in the govi.

The hunsi lie down on the mats. They are covered completely by a white sheet. The mambo begins to shake her asson. She is calling for the spirits of the dead to come from their watery depths.

One at a time they appear. That is, their voices are heard. The voices seem to be gurgling in the water of the mambo's trough. The voices are recognized by the families of the deceased. They call out to them. Sometimes there is a discussion between the gros-bon-ange and its family. Sometimes a gros-bon-ange will complain of past treatment. Sometimes the spirit will express concern about the welfare of its family.

The ceremony and the voices may go on for hours, and all the time the mambo will be shaking her rattle. She will shake the rattle until the last of the gros-bon-ange has traveled the waters, spoken, and entered a govi. Then, and only then, will the sound of mambo's asson stop.

The hunsi carry the govi, heavier with the weight of the gros-bon-ange, into the humfort and arrange them around the altar. They are to remain there until the evening or the day after, when they will be burned.

Even after the funeral, the rites for the dead are not quite finished. In voodoo, these rites are never finished. The dead have simply taken their place with the loa and the marassa to form the voodoo trinity, to be attended, respected, feared and worshiped.

Rada Loa and Petro Loa

Generally, all the loa of the voodoo pantheon are either

A woman possessed by a Petro loa holds her feet atop a red-hot iron post.

Rada loa or Petro loa. One explanation of the differences between the two groups is that Rada loa have clear African origins whereas Petro loa were "created" in Haiti. The word Rada is the corruption of Allada, an area in Dahomey. The origin of Petro is more colorful. Legend has it that at one time in Haiti there was a powerful and evil priest whose name was Dom Pedro. It is said that he did not give up his soul to God when he died. Dom Pedro died with the spirit of the loa in his head. According to voodoo beliefs and traditions, people who die this way become loa themselves. It was this Dom Pedro who became the first of the Petro gods. Since he had been a priest given to evil, it followed that he became an evil and wicked loa.

It would seem to follow that all Petro gods deal in harm and mischief and that all Rada gods perform nothing but good. This is not the case. There is, however, one marked difference between worship in the two groups. Petro ceremonies are likely to demand more violent ritual, such as walking and dancing on hot embers, or the thrusting of a hand into a blazing fire. While Rada worship is not entirely without such performances, they are not so common.

Voodoo Hierarchy

Other faiths, other cultures, have had their pantheons of gods—Greece, Rome, Egypt, the Germanic tribes—and each has had one god more mighty than all the others. For the ancient Greeks it was Zeus, ruler over heaven and earth. For the ancient Romans it was Jupiter, or Jove. Odin and Thor were the first among the Germanic gods, and for the ancient Egyptians it was Re, or Amun.

In voodoo, there is no mightiest or more powerful god. There is nothing resembling a hierarchy in the great list of voodoo deities, as there is no hierarchy in its priesthood. On the contrary, each of the loa has his or her own sphere of influence which governs an integral part of the lives of their worshipers.

4

THE TEMPLES OF THE GODS

Daily voodoo rituals are generally simple. They may be no more than the act of offering a little food or drink to the loa of the house, the family deity. This is all that the overwhelming number of faithful can afford. More elaborate rites are celebrated in the "maison de servitude" (a place for private worship), the "caille mystères" (the house of gods), the "tonnelle" (a peristyle, a roof supported by columns), and the "humfort" (the sanctuary of the voodoo priest, "hungan," or priestess, "mambo").

Where the worshipers are poor, the maison de servitude may be a small unpainted cabin, built of the rudest materials. The wealthier congregations construct sturdier houses of worship and decorate the walls with pictures of flowers, snakes and other voodoo symbols.

In these wealthier constructions, there are generally two entrances to two separate rooms. One of the rooms is dedicated to the loa, the other to the spirits of the dead, and the twins. Where the congregations are richest—or the hungan or mambo are especially important people—there may be additional rooms in the house: one room for the Rada gods, another for the Petro gods, a third for the deities of other voodoo categories.

In each room—whatever the size of the maison de servitude—a platform two or three feet tall, is erected against one of the walls. On this platform the faithful place their offerings of food to the gods on plates which have been fashioned from the wood of calabash trees. There is also a special plate on the platform for a thunderstone and a necklace. The thunderstone has secret voodoo significance. The necklace is for the snake god Damballa.

The humfort, not to be confused with the maison de servitude, is the center for voodoo ritual. It is the temple of the voodoo gods, over which the hungan or mambo presides. The humfort proper is usually a square-shaped house with a holy inner sanctum. A peristyle is usually attached to the house. The peristyle, except for its roof, is open to the elements. Most often, there is also a large completely open area surrounding the house and peristyle. This area is used in different ways for different rites. Ordinarily the sacrificial animals wander in this area. Sometimes, because of the pigs, goats, chickens, and ducks, it is difficult to distinguish the sacred house from a farmhouse.

The humfort has several rooms, the number depending on the wealth and status of the hungan or mambo. Each of the rooms is reserved for the worship of one or a number of gods. The walls of the rooms are decorated with the proper "verver" (mystic ritual design) and there is an altar for each god worshiped. The altars are decorated with plates for the gods, necklaces, thunderstones, crosses, and, sometimes, the cards the hungan employs for divining purposes. There is also a special, secret room where acolytes endure a variety of secret rites before they become full-fledged members of their cult.

The peristyle is no more than a flat tin or brush roof, supported by a number of well-placed wooden posts, but it is a sturdy structure. It needs to be as much of voodoo

A voodoo peristyle. On the rear wall are painted the symbols of the powers that protect the humfort.

ritual takes place here. Its roof must be strong enough to hold a celebrant who, "possessed" by some god, might climb up on it.

The center post of the peristyle, called the "porto mita" or the "poteau-mitan" or the "porto cabesse," is perhaps its most important feature. The loa rest in the poteau-mitan until they are summoned to the voodoo ritual by chanting and the beating of drums. This post is generally decorated with a variety of voodoo snake patterns in homage to the snake god Damballa and to his wife, Aida-Wedo, who is also a snake loa. The more important rites of the voodoo ceremonials revolve around the poteau-mitan. In certain areas of voodoo practice, a whip is frequently attached to the sacred pole. The whip is presumably a symbol for both penitence and redemption for the faithful. There may also be notches cut into the poteau-mitan, in which the celebrants may place food or some other offering.

A number of other symbols of worship are usually hung from the crossbeams of the peristyle. There may be calabashes, baskets and trays, flags, and pictures of saints. A little distance from the peristyle, a bonfire is kept burning to honor one or another of the gods in the voodoo pantheon. Usually, but not always, the god is Legba.

The trees surrounding the entire humfort are often painted and decorated with the colors and the symbols of the gods. These trees, it is believed, are the homes of the gods. The trees themselves are included among the voodoo deities. At the foot of each tree there is a place to put consecrated food.

The hungan or mambo preside over the humfort and all the ceremonies. They are the most highly respected people in their communities because of their knowledge and wisdom. The faithful believe that the hungan and mambo have been given their knowledge and wisdom by the spirits of the ancestors and the spirit of the marassa. Since the voodoo believer thinks that daily life is controlled by one deity or another, the knowledge and wisdom of the voodoo priests is constantly sought and always respected.

Even people who have successful businesses will ask the hungan for financial advice. Politicians and others of high rank will seek the counsel of their hungans. The hungan will be questioned about a possible marriage partner or a family quarrel, or will be asked to cure a disease, save a child from dying, or locate an evil wanga. He is the doctor, the confessor, the magician, as well as the priest of his congregation. He is indeed a very busy man (or woman if she is a mambo), but he must also be very wise and know his gods and congregation well enough to keep them both happy. For, if he fails his people, they will conclude that he has failed the gods and is losing or has already lost their knowledge and wisdom. In such a case, he will quickly lose not only his standing as an hungan, but his congregation as well.

The hungan does not operate alone. He has a number of assistants who are of different rank and perform a variety of functions during the religious ceremonies.

First there is the apprentice hungan or mambo, who is called the confiance. Such an individual is the confidant of the voodoo priest—a sort of right-hand man, or woman, as the case may be.

The "house hungenikon" (hungenikon caille) is another helper. This person takes care of the humfort to see that everything is in its proper place and in proper order.

The hungenikon peristyle is the voodoo disciple who leads the singing of chants at the voodoo ceremonies. He can stop and start them when he sees fit.

The leader of the parades at the voodoo rites, the master of ceremonies, is called la-place. It is the la-place who, sword or machete in his hand, leads whatever procession takes place during a voodoo ritual.

The *reine silence* (queen silence) acts in the manner of a sergeant-at-arms at voodoo rites by maintaining a quiet atmosphere among the celebrants.

There are also specially assigned individuals who procure the animals which are to be sacrificed, and others whose job it is to prepare and cook the slaughtered animals. There is also a quarter-master hungenikon whose job it is to divide the sacrificed animals between the gods and the celebrants. The quarter-master also distributes among the faithful the food which has not been eaten by the gods.

All hungans and mambos do not have so many assistants.

A mambo leading a ceremonial invocation. Traditionally, the ritual clothing for a voodoo priestess is made of satin.

The size of the retinue, of course, depends on the individual wealth and power of the priest. But every humfort has its "hunsi." Sometimes the male hunsi are called "adjanikon." The hunsi are general assistants to the hungan or mambo, and form the chorus of singers in the voodoo chanting. As apprentices, it is their task to take over the ritual whenever their hungan or mambo is possessed by a loa and goes into a trance.

Some of these apprentices are "hunsi kanzo." These are the faithful who have undergone an ordeal by fire in their initiation.

The musicians attached to a humfort have special titles too. The trianglier plays the triangle. The ogantier plays the ogan (usually the blade of a hoe and a spike). The drummers are grouped under the name of huntorguiers, but each has his own separate title. The man who beats the big drum, the manman, is called the manmanier. The one who beats the seconde, the middle-sized drum, is called the secondier. The one beating the smallest drum, the bula, is named the bulaier.

Finally, around each humfort, there is an organization of people, not voodoo initiates, whose purpose it is to be of aid both to the humfort and the congregation. It is much like any of the number of societies which are organized around churches all over the world. They are meant to help the church or temple but, primarily, their function is of a social nature.

These voodoo organizations, like the others, have their officers. In the voodoo society these include a president, vice-president, ministers, deputies, senators and commanders. The functions of each varies, but the society as a whole is involved in preparing social functions as well as humfort ceremonies. Like a fraternity or sorority, the organization is concerned with the well-being of its membership. It will assist in case of financial distress, it will attend members who have become ill, it will comfort the bereaved and help defray the cost of burials for those who are perhaps too poor to pay for the proper rites.

At one time these voodoo social organizations were quite powerful, politically as well as socially. Time, however, has diminished much of their influence.

The temple of the voodoo gods, then, may be seen as not only a place of worship, but also as a center of all voodoo life. It is a complex organization that has control over much, if not all, of the life around it.

5

INITIATION

There are two classes of hunsi who live in or around the humfort: hunsi bossal and hunsi kanso. The hunsi bossal are assigned menial tasks. Their work is usually household chores, such as sweeping, washing, and cleaning. The hunsi kanzo have undergone rigid training and initiation, sometimes by fire, and they assist the hungan during ceremonies and rituals.

Candidates for hunsi kanzo training and initiation are chosen by the hungan. Training may take years. The hunsi kanzo must be thoroughly versed in all voodoo rites and dances and know all the voodoo gods of the humfort, their names, what they wear, their way of walking and talking, and all their individual characteristics. Preparation for the initiation itself requires several weeks of demanding practice. The initiation itself can take six or seven days, depending on the traditions and practices of the humfort.

To prepare themselves for the beginning of the long initiation ritual candidates will make frequent visits to the churches in the area, primarily for confession. They will take many baths in water made sacred by an infusion of special leaves. They will not eat or drink anything which might tend either to dull their senses or excite them.

The hungan selects the day for the beginning of the initiation, but keeps it secret for fear that some evil wanga may be cast on the proceedings. On the appointed day, the candidates will gather in the humfort to begin their long and arduous ordeal.

They drape palm leaves around their shoulders and in front of their faces. They dance, and chant a canticle to the loa Aizan, said to be the oldest of the voodoo deities. As they sing and dance, they tear the palm leaves into strips, which they then plait into whips. They chant—

"Aizan is a loa.
Tear the aizan.
Aizan listen."

The bush priests baptizes the whips and blesses them—the Church is rarely if ever forgotten in voodoo rites. The hungenikon, the choir leader, then picks up the whips (called "aizan") and dances with them. First, he dances around the poteau-mitan, then he moves to the doors of the various rooms in the humfort, and finally to the sacred trees outside the peristyle under which the ceremony is being conducted. He returns, then, to the peristyle, where he offers the aizan to the hungan to be kissed, then to the hunsi and to any spectators who might be present. They make similar gestures of respect and devotion. These rituals done, the hungenikon departs with the aizan and deposits them carefully in the room in which the novices will soon be sequestered.

The second ritual is more like an open class in voodoo practice. The huño, as the candidates are called, go through the routine of rites and dances they have been taught until the hungan or mambo is completely satisfied with their performance.

The huño are then made to lie down all around the

poteau-mitan on their backs. This done, the hungan or mambo pours water into each of their mouths, then makes a cross of some powdered substance on the candidate's face, chest and palms. After this, the hungan or mambo whips each of their legs and scolds them—probably for some real or imagined wrongdoing in the past. Then, with a sacred rattle, the hungan or mambo taps the candidates on their mouths, cheeks or forehead. Finally, the candidates get up from the ground.

Next, a large stone is placed on the head of each candidate, and they begin a processional dance which takes them around the poteau-mitan and out to the sacred trees while the hungan or mambo and hunsi sing. Then there is a short speech by the hungan, in the nature of a pep talk, admonishing the huño never to forget their responsibilities. Then the candidates, singly or by twos, approach the hungan and kiss the ground before him. Then the hungan spins each candidate around in a little circle. Taking off their shoes, they approach the hungan again, and each is kissed on the mouth by the priest who shows signs of deep mourning.

Mourning suddenly takes over the entire ceremony, all its participants and even those who are just spectators. Everyone begins to moan and weep. Symbolically, the ritual has become one of death. Symbolically, the huño are dying. Eventually they will be symbolically resurrected. What we are witnessing is one more variation of the ancient rites of death and resurrection.

We do not know the beginnings of such rites but it is likely that prehistoric man celebrated such a death and resurrection ritual, most likely inspired by the cycle of the seasons, the "death and the resurrection" of the grain which fed him. We know that the ancient Sumerians mourned the death of their god Tammuz and celebrated his return to life. The Greek Adonis was, with defined regularity, killed by a boar and resurrected in the form of the anemone—a spring flower. Similarly, the Egyptian god Osiris was destroyed and reborn. In the Christian Church there is the Crucifixion and Resurrection of Christ.

As the sounds of mourning and weeping increase in volume, bandages are tied around the eyes of the huño. This done, the candidates are symbolically dead. Then they are rudely pushed and shoved into the "djevo," the secret initiation room. Symbolically the huño are being buried. They will remain in the djevo until the final day of the initiation rites, when they will come out reborn (resurrected) as hunsi kanzo.

The djevo has already been prepared for the entrance of the huño. The hungan has already spread the "verver," sacred designs drawn in flour on the floor. Mats, generally made of straw, have been placed over these verver. Each huño will rest on a mat for the next seven days.

Before the candidates take their beds, each is dressed in a simple white tunic and sits on a bed of sacred leaves while the hungan cuts a lock of hair from the huño's head and from other parts of the body. Nails are then pared from the huño's left hand and left foot. The hair and nail parings are wrapped in a banana leaf along with some grilled corn, feathers plucked from sacrificed chickens, and some sweetened starchy liquid. The whole creation is placed in pots which will remain with the huño in the djevo for the entire period of the "retreat."

Following the final rites, the hungan keeps the pots on an altar in the house of worship. The hungan uses the pots to protect the soon-to-be hunsi kanzo against evil forces. It is also the hungan's way of ensuring good behavior and obedience from his future hunsi kanzo.

A second head-washing, *lavé tete* as it is called, then fol-

Verver, sacred voodoo designs drawn in flour

lows. This lavé tete is somewhat more complicated than the head-washing which is done the first time a person is possessed by a loa (see chapter 7). For this second lavé tete the huño's head is washed with water which has been made sacred with a mixture of sacred leaves. Then a mixture made of wine-soaked bread, a variety of mashed grains, and the blood of sacrificed fowl and animals is wrapped in sacred leaves, then in a kerchief. The kerchief is wrapped around the head and the eyes of the huño. The kerchief will remain tied and untouched until the initiation is over. The huño may do nothing to remove or even counteract the foul odor which develops in the kerchief. He must endure the foul smell until he becomes, officially, a hunsi kanzo.

Following this head-washing ceremony and the binding

of the kerchief, the huño moves to his mat, kisses the ground before it, then lies down on his bed on his left side. His pillow is generally a stone atop a few coins of small denomination. The candidate is covered by a sheet.

During the entire week of this sacred retreat, the candidate is expected not to move or speak without special permission. He may not laugh. Symbolically, the djevo has become his tomb. There are only three times during the day when these strict rules are relaxed at all: in the morning when the huño washes himself and twice when he is rubbed down with sacred oils. At such times, the huño is permitted to sit up on his straw mat for a few minutes, or to turn himself in his bed. As to the normal bodily functions, some authorities say he may leave his djevo in the darkness of the early morning, while others say that he may not leave for any reason at all until the last day of his initiation.

As to food, the only meat the huño may eat is chicken, and then only the least savory parts such as head, feet, and tripe. The meat is never seasoned or salted. His drink is limited almost entirely to water. This strict diet is carefully managed and supervised by a specially chosen woman. She must belong to the humfort, be a hunsi kanzo, and hold the complete trust of the hungan. The huño does have a bell, or a rattle, with which to summon help in the event of an emergency.

The evening before the retreat comes to a close, there is a special celebration in honor of the candidates' mait-tete—the first loa to possess them. All the favorite foods and beverages of the different loa are prepared. The hungan draws the sacred verver of each of the gods with flour on the floor of the djevo. He covers the verver with mats upon which he places the offerings.

The candidates sit on the floor, their legs apart. The

hungan or mambo approaches them, drops handfuls of the food upon their heads, and sprinkles their heads with water, sweet kola or some other drink, depending on the taste of each huño's mait-tete. Next, the hungan or mambo moves to the novice with a chicken the candidate has previously given him or her. The bird is induced to peck at the candidate's mouth and hands.

If the hen pecks as it is expected to, then the hungan reads it as a sign that all has gone well. He gives the fowl to the huño who holds the bird to his breast. This done, the hungan retrieves the bird, breaks its wings and legs, tears out its tongue—sometimes with the teeth—then lets three drops of the chicken's blood fall on the huñso's head.

The hungan then kills the bird by wringing its neck. Some of its feathers are pulled out and stuck—with the blood of the chicken—to the candidate's head and to the sacred pot containing hair and nail parings. The hungan uses blood from the chicken to draw a cross on the nape of the huñso's neck, forehead, left palm and the bottom of the left foot.

Throughout the rites the candidates are considered possessed by their loa so it is the gods—not the human candidates—who are receiving so much attention during the initiation. In fact, the candidate will not remember any of the ceremonies. The candidate will not recall chanting, "The loa wants something to eat," as the hungan put the food into his mouth. Nor will he remember that the hungan also put some of the food for his god between the big toe and the second toe of his left foot, as he sang, "A loa in a pot cannot eat. You must do the eating for him."

The last two rituals the acolyte must celebrate in the hunsi kanzo rites are the ceremony of the *bulé-zin* (burning pots) and the final baptism.

Canticles to Legba begin the ceremonials. There is an

elaborate ceremony of greetings with the hungan saluting the hunsi who are present—not the candidates. They are still sequestered in the djevo. The hunsi who are present greet the hungan, then each other, then spin each other around in a little circle. Then the la-place, the voodoo master of ceremonies, enters leading a group of flag bearers. Each flag is greeted ceremoniously and kissed by all those assembled for the ritual in the peristyle.

The hungan's chief assistant, the confiance of the humfort, enters wearing the necklaces of the hunsi around his neck and arms. The power of these sacred ornaments is so overwhelming that the confiance reels and staggers, falls to his knees while the ogantier hammers his ogan, the drummers beat their drums and the hungan shakes his rattle.

The hungan removes the sacred necklaces from the confiance. Each of the hunsi moves to the hungan and kneels while the hungan places a necklace on each.

The hunsi then bring in the candidates' sacred pots along with plates and food especially prepared for the ritual. The hunsi parade in the peristyle following the confiance, who waves two chickens above his head. The hunsi carry the pots, plates, and food on their heads. And they dance and jump along until, at a given command, each kneels to put down the burden in its special place. Finally, each hunsi takes his or her assigned seat. All this is done to the sound of drums and chanting.

At this point the hungan speaks Catholic prayers. He begins with the Paternoster, Ave Maria, and Credo. These are for the mightiest God, the Catholic God. He moves from prayers to Catholic psalms, and finally to pure voodoo chants. This is followed immediately by more hunsi dancing, this time around the poteau-mitan. Then the dancing stops and the rites involving the pots and the food begin.

The hunsi take off their shoes. They each take three pegs, go through the ritual of pointing the pegs to the four points of the compass. This done, they drive the pegs into the ground in the form of triangles. They place the pot on the pegs, then light fire to the pegs.

They then take two chickens each, point these to the north, south, east and west, then break their wings and legs, pull off their heads, pluck, singe, and cut them up. They wash the pieces of chicken, then drop them in water which is already boiling.

Everything has now been done for the entrance of the candidates from their seclusion in the djevo. The huño have washed themselves and have been fed some kind of sedative. They emerge, wrapped in their sheets from head to foot, led by the more important personages of the hum-fort, and singing quietly the songs which the hunsi are chanting in the peristyle.

The huños are now ready for the ordeal by fire. This element of the ritual is not nearly as dangerous as it seems, nor is it intended to be. First the candidate soaks his hand in a mixture of oil and wine. The oil is thick enough to prevent any serious burn. Three times the candidate puts his hand in the mixture, then touches his palm to the ground. Then, three times the huño grasps a handful of hot corn flour. Following this he passes his left hand through the fire which comes up from the burning pot. The rite itself is expected to bring the huño luck, good health and certain magical powers.

Other rites follow, but the huños are not involved in them. There is more dancing, the pots are burned so hot that they break, then the pot and some special sticks are broken up and thrown into a hole. The dancing will continue till the sun rises, and perhaps longer.

Later, usually on a Sunday morning, the la-place leads the huños from the djevo. The candidates are dressed in white and wear straw hats over their kerchiefed heads and strips of aizan before their faces. Under a white sheet, held up by the hunsi, they move to the sacred trees which house their different gods and salute them. This done, they are returned to the peristyle where the hungan or the mambo gives them a final lecture on the advantages, obligations, and duties of the hunsi kanzo.

Later that day, generally during the afternoon, the novices once more emerge from the djevo. They humbly salute the door of the djevo, the poteau-mitan, the flags and symbols, the hungan, all persons of rank, and the drums as well, since they are sacred instruments. They then proceed, each huño holding a candle, to the altar in the peristyle. The bush priest reads the Church prayers, then sprinkles the holy water on the huños' heads. At this point the huño becomes a full-fledged hunsi kanzo.

The celebration begins again. The drums beat, the dancers dance, the faithful from time to time are possessed. It is a religious and magic festival, celebrating resurrection.

These initiation rites, like all other voodoo rituals, are rarely the same in any two regions, in any two humforts. Generally, however, they follow this pattern. Symbolically the novice dies, is buried, and then is reborn.

The initiation rites for the elevation of voodoo worshipers to the position of hungan, or mambo, are similar to the rituals involved in the creation of the hunsi kanzo. As may be expected, they are of longer duration and more demanding of the candidate.

First there is the call, much as it comes in other faiths.

The call may come by visitation of the loa in dreams. It may come in the course of a man's or woman's possession. However it comes, the voodoo adherent must answer it, even if he fears the burdens and responsibilities such calling demands. Of course, because of the respect and power the hungan and mambo holds in voodoo society there are some who seek to become priests without the call. These men and women are said to have "bought" the loa. They become "double-dealers" or bocors, dealers in black magic.

Whatever the case, the candidate for the "asson," the sacred rattle of the hungan, approaches the voodoo priest of his choice and requests an apprenticeship. This apprenticeship will carry the candidate through the ranks of a humfort: hunsi, hunsi kanzo, hungenikon, and confiance, before he is ready to undergo his final initiation rites.

The asson is made of a calabash covered by a net into which are sewn beads, small stones, and the vertebrae of snakes. It will be baptized before it becomes the sacred symbol of the priesthood. The candidate will carry the unbaptized asson with him into the solitude of his djevo, but only when the hungan deems the time is right. The candidate will remain in the djevo for a period of seven to twenty-one days. The length of time will depend on the mystic readings of the hungan.

In substance, the ordeals in the djevo for the asson candidate are those of the hunsi kanzo: the need to lie on his left side, the prohibition against movement, and so on. There is a deck of cards added to the few coins under the stone pillow of the candidate. This may seem odd, but it isn't. The hungan is expected to see omens in his cards and to make predictions from his reading of them. In a number of humforts, the candidate's head is shaved. Or there is the ceremony in which the candidate must lie entirely naked and swear an oath, dedicating him or herself to the service of the loa, and swearing never to reveal anything which has gone on during his or her initiation.

The final rites, creating the hungan or mambo, are rather universal throughout the world of voodoo. The candidate is lifted, while he sits in an armchair, three times. The ritual is called, simply, *haussement,* which in English reads "lifting." To the general acclamation of all present, the candidate is declared hungan or mambo. He or she may now build a humfort.

6

VOODOO WORSHIP

Voodoo ritual may be simple or, as we have seen, complex. Ordinarily, the faithful will light a candle, throw some water libation in the place of worship, and this will be enough to satisfy the loa. Sometimes a handful of grain, some pieces of meat, called the mangé sec, are added to the devotion. The voodoo worshiper must be certain that the gods are at all times pleased with the services tended them. If the loa feel neglected, the worshiper, it is believed, is certain to be visited by some misfortune sent by a petulant or angry loa.

If a member of the voodoo faithful suffers a series of misfortunes such as crop failure, misadventure in business, unexpected deaths, then the worshiper's services to the loa have been insufficient or, worse, some evil magician has cast a spell. The hungan or mambo can summon the loa, and it is the loa who will reveal the cause for the bad fortune.

The devotee also consults the hungan or mambo about daily life decisions. The person may simply want advice from the gods about the best day to start on a journey or the best approach to a young lady. For whatever reason the mambo is approached, the ritual she performs is the same.

The mambo shuts herself up in her sanctuary. The petitioner remains outside its door but can hear everything that goes on in the sanctuary.

The mambo rattles her asson. She speaks the Latin of the Catholic prayers, then the unintelligible phrases which are understood to be the language of the loa.

There is an abrupt change in the tone of the voice which comes from the sanctuary. There will be several such changes as, presumably, different loa come from the govi jar which the mambo has been addressing.

Each of the loa will be recognized by the petitioner. Each loa has a different manner of speech and the devotee knows that difference in the rhythm, tone, pitch, of each god's voice. Nevertheless, the mambo will repeat the message of the loa and interpret it. There will be advice, perhaps caution, perhaps admonition. There may be requests and demands. The session ends. The mambo emerges from her sanctuary.

The devotee knows what is expected. If the loa have been displeased, they may demand a sacrifice. If such is the case, the faithful voodoo adherent has a rather large and costly task ahead. If the devotee neglects his obligation, his misfortunes are certain to increase. If he tries to put it off, the loa will come to him in his dreams to remind him of his duties. Or, at one time or another, in the variety of voodoo ceremonies, the gods will possess other believers and, through them, scold and harass the devotee, perhaps threaten him with dire consequences for his neglect.

Actually the loa do not often request a particularly huge demonstration of devotion. Perhaps once every ten or fifteen years a family may get together to finance an elaborate service. Even for large families such ceremonies may prove very expensive. There is the priest or the priestess to be paid, as well as his or her large retinue of assistants. A bush priest is also required. The drummers and the other instrumentalists are costly, and so is the ritual food and the animals to be sacrificed.

Most voodooists are poor. They have no choice but to do without most of this ritual paraphernalia. A man's tiny hut is often the only house of worship he can afford. He will make an altar of the one table he possesses, cover it with a simple white cloth, and place his meager offerings to the gods upon it. He will have the sacred symbols drawn on the dirt floor of his hut, but will have only a few candles to light around it. There will be no drums or other sacred instruments because he cannot afford to pay for them. Nor can he pay for the services of a hungan or a mambo. He will conduct the rituals himself and call on his relatives and friends to perform the duties of the assistants.

The service conducted at a humfort for a person of means—or a person who has been able to borrow the necessary funds—will be markedly different. It will be an elaborate and sumptuous series of rites that may last seven days and more. The extent of its splendor and duration will be limited only by the amount of money the person can spend.

For an elaborate service an oil lamp, usually a floating wick in a container of palm oil, in addition to the candles is placed on the altar. There will also be a crucifix, a bowl of holy water, rice cooked in milk, a porridge of rice and beans, cooked chicken, a variety of beverages from kola to coffee, and all kinds of fruits and syrups.

The white cloth which covers the altar will be decorated with colored lithographs of the Catholic saints. Outside the humfort a bonfire dedicated to the god Legba will be kept burning. There will be one kind of decoration or another in the trees which surround the peristyle, the trees in which the gods reside. The fowl and the animals to be sacrificed: chickens, turkeys, pigeons, pigs, goats, perhaps a bull (if there is that much money in the family) will be tethered among the trees.

When the family and its guests are all assembled in the peristyle, the hungan opens the ceremonies. He takes a jug of water and points it to the four cardinal points of the compass. This is the salute to Legba, without whose permission no other gods may appear. The hungan also salutes the three principal spirits of the voodoo world, the loas, the dead, and the twins. The three other points to which the hungan points his jug of water may also represent the Holy Trinity—God, Jesus, and the Holy Spirit, for it is necessary for a voodoo celebration to invoke the approval and blessings of the Church.

The jug is then carried to one of the entrances to the peristyle, where the hungan spills some of its water three times as an offering to the gods. He repeats the ritual at two other entrances to the sacred enclosure, each time drawing a line of water to the poteau-mitan. It is on these three streams, since the loa are presumed to travel on water, that the gods will come to the celebrants. Each important person present repeats the ceremony of the jug, taking turns pouring the libations, making the streams.

The bush priest, always present at such ceremonies, brings the Church into the voodoo rites. He begins his part in the rituals by chanting the Catholic hymns familiar to the congregation. All kneel on the ground as he recites the Paternoster, the Ave Maria, and the Credo. During this phase of the ceremonies, called the *action de grace,* the voodoo flag-bearers parade around the celebrants. At times, urged to show a bit more enthusiasm in their exercise, the flag-bearers step up their pace, go into a kind of

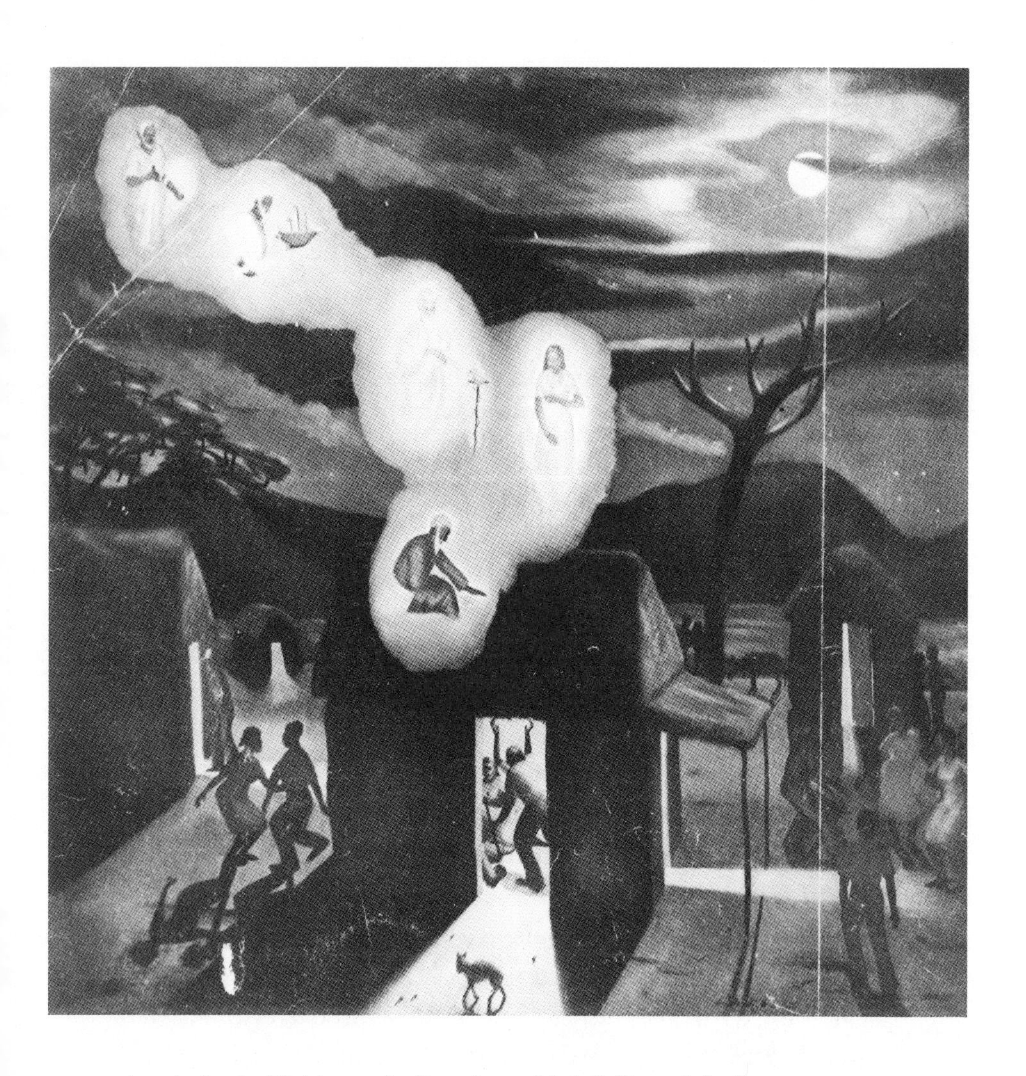

A painting by Haitian artist Benedetto titled *Calling of the Loa*

dançe. As the bush priest recites the "adoration," the family conducting the service gives him coins and candles. Following his benediction comes the Christian chant, a hymn the congregation joins in singing. Slowly but definitely the hymn takes on a voodoo sound. The hungan takes over and the bush priest fades into the background.

First the hungan calls on the different family members to

speak to their loa. They are encouraged to speak of their particular difficulties, unpleasant encounters, unhappy experiences. The loa urges them to express their wishes and desires.

Next, an assistant takes six candles to the hungan, then parades around the ceremonial grounds with them before placing four of them behind the sacred altar at the cardinal points—north, south, east and west. The members of the family place lighted candles within the circumference created by the assistants.

This done, the hungan draws the sacred verver on the ground. He then proceeds to summon the loa by ringing a bell and blowing a whistle. He orders a basin of water placed before the altar, in which to wash the sacrificial animals. He becomes possessed.

The singing continues. The sacrificial animals are washed—sometimes their whole bodies, sometimes just their feet. Following the washing, they are carefully dried, perfumed, powdered, even decorated with ribbons. To be offered to the gods, they must be clean and presented in elegant attire.

The fowl and the animals are then escorted to the verver, on which has been set three plates—one with corn meal, one with gray ashes, one with a mixture of roasted coffee beans. The animals eat the food and this is considered a good omen. The omen means the gods are pleased with the potential sacrifice. They are in attendance at the ritual. They begin to "ride" their "horses." The congregation is possessed.

The singing continues.

"Where is Erzilie?
The food is ready."
"He found something on the ground.

Do not pick it up."
"I am worried.
I am worried today, Baron Samedi."

It is time for the sacrifice. Slowly, one by one, the hungan brings the possessed back to themselves.

The singing continues.

He makes the sign of the cross over each animal, then each is killed with the stroke of a knife, or a machete, and its blood collected in sacred bowls.

Sometimes the sacrifice is more ornate. Once the animals and fowl have eaten the sacred food, they become the property of the gods. Belonging to the gods, they become sacred, and must be treated accordingly. If it is a goat to be sacrificed, members of the congregation may kneel before it, rub foreheads with it, kiss the ground before it. At times such rituals are more mystic, particularly among possessed attendants at the rites. A man may ride an animal, or suck at its muzzle, or put his mouth to the muzzle of an animal as if inhaling its breath—its spirit. The reason for this behavior seems to be the devotee's need to get as close as possible to the sacred loa.

The singing continues.

The hungan makes the sign of the cross over the bodies of the sacrificed animals which are then carried away to be cleaned and cooked. The bowl of blood is placed on the altar.

The head, feet, intestines and other parts of the animals less appreciated as food, are separated and prepared for the unfriendly gods, the gods who are to be "restrained." This food, together with thread and a number of needles whose eyes have been broken is placed into a numbers of jars, one jar for each unfriendly loa. The jars are buried with the proper invocation in song—

"Go away from here.
This is not your country."

The eyes of the needles are broken with a purpose. The unfriendly loa are expected to be kept busy for a number of years, trying to thread the needles—an impossible task, since the needles have no eyes. The offering of food, poor though it is, rids the family of any further obligation to the unfriendly loa. Sometimes an iron cross is buried with these jars. According to voodoo belief, this gives the family further assurance that they are finally rid of the malevolent gods. A giant wooden cross, as a rule, is planted over this "grave site."

The rituals of the first day usually end with this burial rite. The second day, the ceremonies begin in much the same way. There is the "action de grace," the pret-savanne chanting the Paternoster, the Ave Maria, the Credo, and leading the prayers, with the hungan taking over as the chanting moves into the voodoo language and rhythm.

Again the hungan draws his sacred designs on the ground. Again the loa are summoned and a good number of the celebrants are possessed by their gods. More fowl and animals are sacrificed in the prescribed tradition: the washing, the dressing, the nibbling and, finally, the sacrificial killing. Possession takes over the entire assembly, and most of the gods worshiped by the congregation make their appearance. Legba dances over the hot embers of the fire which has been created for him. Erzilie is the queenly flirt. Damballa rolls in the mud. Gede prattles through his nose, dispensing his usual gossip. The hungan and his assistants try to quiet those possessed who have become too violent in their gestures. Damballa is removed so that he may clean himself up and change his clothes.

There is more sacrifice. There is more singing. It is in the early hours of the next morning before those responsible for preparing and cooking the sacrificed animals are ready to serve them.

The hungan prepares the food-service for each of the loa to be served. He gives each member of the family a plate and lines up the congregation, in twos, before the house of worship. He intones the Catholic prayers, then announces that the food is ready and invites the gods (possessed celebrants) to come and eat.

The table is well set with eating utensils, salt, pepper and other spices. The members of the family then enter and place the plates of food on the table. Their task done, they leave the house of worship. The door is closed. The gods are eating and all wait, more or less patiently, for perhaps hours, while the loa feast on the offerings made to them.

The final act of the ritual comes when the hungan knocks at the door of the house of worship and enters the room to ask whether the gods are done with their dining. The act is a formality. The loa have been sated with the offerings: meats, grains, and beverages. The hungan invites the family to join him in the house of worship. They enter, take their place at the table, and consume what food and drink the gods have left them.

The dance, which is always part of the ceremonies, follows on a Saturday night. The government authorities will not issue permits for such dances on any day of the week but Saturday. The dance ends on Sunday morning in time for the voodoo celebrants to go home, get changed and get to Sunday mass in their Catholic churches on time. The Saturday voodoo dance and the Sunday mass assure the faithful that neither God nor his loa is being neglected.

The service described lasted three to four days. Sometimes, however, the opening ceremonies led by the pret-savanne may take an entire day. Sometimes the sacrifices are more elaborate. In these cases the service may take as much as a week.

There are other variations of this service, depending on the area in which it is celebrated, depending on the character and the preferences of the hungan who leads it, depending on whether it is a Rada or a Petro ceremony. By and large, however, the manner in which the rites and rituals are introduced, developed, and carried to their conclusions is much the same.

The one element in voodoo worship yet to be explored is the rumored sacrifice of the "goat without horns," a euphemism for a human sacrifice. Human sacrifice to the gods was probably not an uncommon act in our prehistoric era. We do know, according to the Holy Bible, that Abraham was ready to sacrifice his son, Isaac, until the Angel of the Lord intervened. We know that Jephthah of Gilead sacrificed his daughter to the Lord. According to Homer, Agamemnon, the leader of the Greeks in the Trojan War, sacrificed his daughter, Iphigenia, to the gods. But we do *not* know, except by hearsay, that there has been a single instance of human sacrifice in voodoo.

7

POSSESSION—HORSES AND RIDERS

The "possession" of an individual by a voodoo god is perhaps the most mysterious and dramatic of all the elements in voodoo. It is perhaps the key to the entire voodoo experience.

Possession, of course, is not limited to voodoo. A number of recent motion pictures and television shows, which involved possession and exorcism, have made that plain enough. The Lady Abbess in William Shakespeare's *Comedy of Errors* inquires, with reference to Antipholus, one of two pair of twins, "How long hath this possession held this man?" Daniel Defoe, who wrote *Moll Flanders,* defined a "possessionist" as one who believed in the possession of man by spirits. In Jewish folklore, the dybbuk is an evil spirit, the soul of a dead man or a dead woman which inhabits the body of a living person. Possession, along with exorcism, has a long history and no one can possibly say when primitive man was first possessed.

In most cases, possession is seen as an unfortunate occurrence. The one possessed is controlled by an evil spirit, an evil power, which has to be exorcised. This is not at all the situation in voodoo. The spirit which enters the body of a voodoo worshiper is always a loa. It may be a hostile loa that is inclined to punish and hurt, but most often it is a benevolent loa which possesses and "rides his horse." The "horse" is the person the god has possessed.

The "horse" may utter a sharp cry or a piercing moan, as the "rider" enters his or her body. The act of possession appears to be both realistic and physical. Generally the worshiper has the feeling of being struck violently, in the nape of the neck, the back, or the legs. The worshiper shivers, shakes, and trembles, and seems to struggle with the loa, perhaps as Jacob of the Old Testament struggled with the angels. He staggers, he reels, he pushes out his hands and his arms in an effort to fight off the loa. He totters, he tends to bang himself against whatever furniture or people may be near him. He moves around in circles, and sometimes falls, and rolls himself violently on the ground.

All of a sudden, he is still. The loa has finally taken full possession. Physically, even emotionally, the worshiper is no longer himself. He is the loa.

The person possessed, now speaking and acting for the loa who is "riding" him, greets the people in his company and, as a rule, asks for the things which have been prepared for him: his special costume (each god has a special costume and favorite colors), the kerchiefs which he will wind around his head and body, his favorite food and drink. Possession may come at any time to any of the celebrants and while the hungan or the mambo do not know who will be possessed or by which loa, they and their assistants are well prepared to satisfy the request of whatever god may appear.

The transformation of man or woman or child, whichever the devotee is, is amazingly complete. If it is Legba who possesses, the worshiper will become the old grandfather, limping as he walks. If it is Ibo, the worshiper may prance around like a dog. If it is L'inglesou, his manner will be stern and harsh. If it is Gede, he will talk through his nose, become garrulous, and gossip about all those assembled.

The age or sex of the possessed worshiper doesn't seem to matter. A man may become possessed by a female god or a woman by a male god. The man becomes feminine in his attitudes and actions, and the woman takes on male characteristics. As for age, a child possessed by Legba becomes the old man. An old man possessed by Maitresse Mombu may dance the gay dances of the goddess as if he were still in the springtime of his years.

Possession usually occurs during a voodoo service, worship or dance. At such times any number of the faithful may become "horses" for the gods. Possession, however, may also take place in the street, in the marketplace, even in church during a mass. The gods, as a matter of fact, may take to "riding" their "horses" anywhere and at any time. The possessed, in such instances, is said to be invested by an undisciplined loa, a "loa bossal." The loa bossal may prove dangerous to the possessed because of its disregard for the physical well-being of the devotee. To "tame" the loa bossal, make him act in a controlled manner, voodoo demands that the god be baptized.

Baptism, too, is an ancient ritual, but voodoo has been touched considerably by Christian rites, particularly Catholic rites. Part of the baptism of the loa is conducted in the Catholic tradition. Mainly, however, the "taming" of the god is carried out in an unquestionably voodoo manner.

For three days, the individual who has experienced her first possession, and whose loa is being baptized, lies alone on her bed, in a room apart from the rest of the family. Her bed has been freshly made with clean sheets and pillowcases. She has also been provided with three changes of

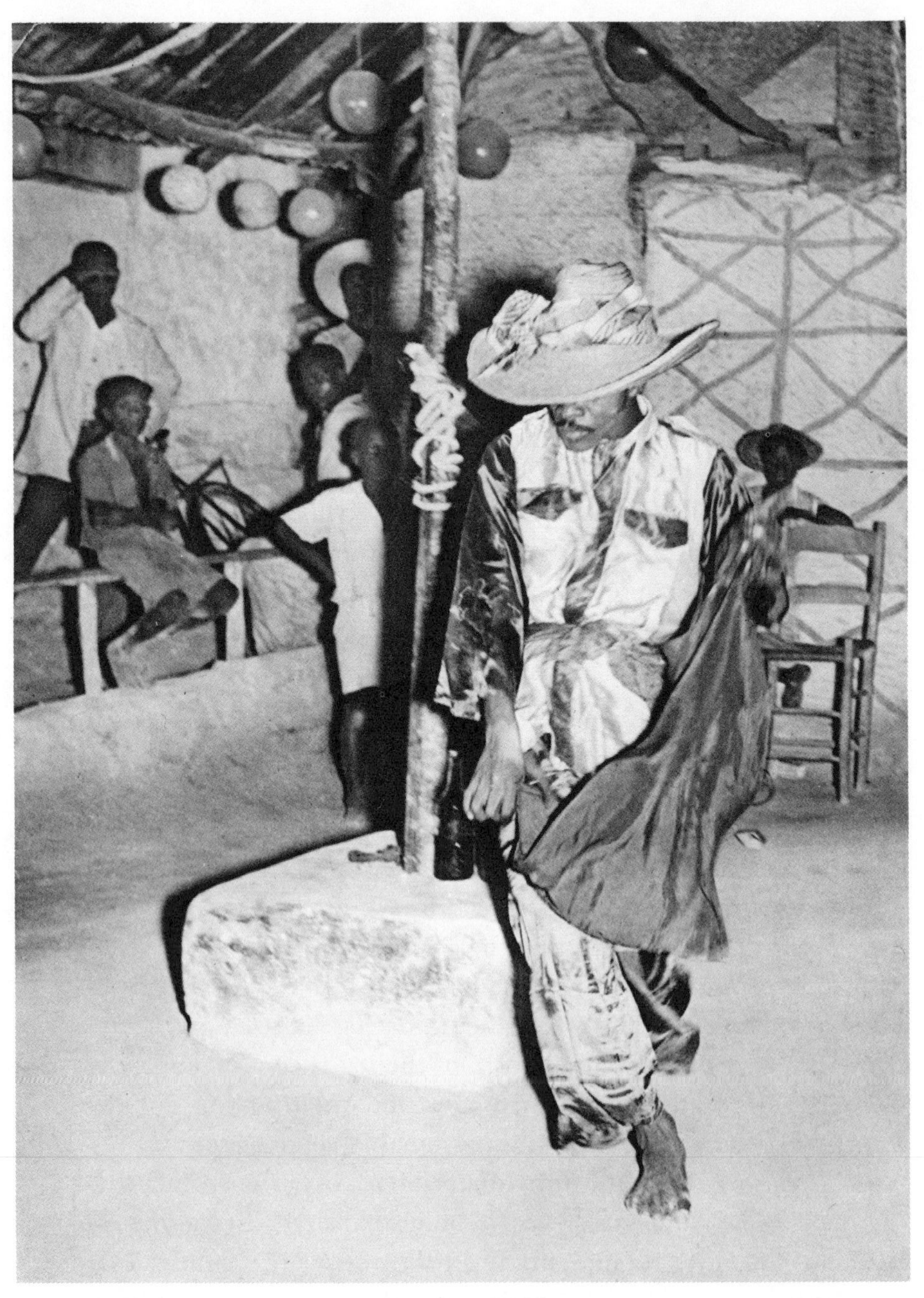

A hungan possessed by the earth god Zaka dances in the peristyle of his humfort.

clothes. One of her dresses, and whatever undergarments she wears, must never have been worn before. If it is a man, one of his suits or shirt and pants must be new. These garments are for the last day of the ritual, when the actual "washing of the head," or baptism, takes place.

While the one who is possessed lies in her bed, the family sings and prays outside the room, or outside the house. The songs and prayers are for the loa who is to be baptized. The Catholic Church is not neglected in the rites. There is usually a member of the family who is pret-savanne, a bush priest, who can read the Catholic prayers, and this person is called on to assist in the rituals. If there's no bush priest in the family, some friendly bush priest is always available. The priest leads the family in prayers and canticles of the Church. Neither God nor the loa is to be forgotten in voodoo rites. The loa is powerful on earth, but God is the more powerful with the natural elements: rain, thunder, rivers, oceans.

Every now and then the family will vary its procedures. They will enter the room where the one who has been possessed lies, and move around in the form of a procession. They will light candles or an oil lamp for the god who is to be baptized. They will give the loa something to drink, most likely the sweet kola. They will offer the god a small sacrifice, some dry offering (*mangé sec*) of the loa's favorite food.

On the third day, a hungan or a mambo, again preferably a member of the family, is called in to officiate at the baptism itself. As in Church ritual, there must also be a godfather and godmother present. To perform rites properly, the hungan or mambo must be in a state of possession, that is, possessed by a god. For the baptism of the loa in possession of the devotee is supposed to be carried out by another loa.

The baptism is done with perfumed water which has had leaves steeped in it. While Church canticles and songs are sung to the loa, the hungan or mambo washes the head of the possessed devotee. As soon as the washing of the head begins, the devotee is again possessed by the loa who was the first to "ride" her, and she falls back on her bed, completely under the control of the god. All the other participants at the baptism fall down to their knees in the manner of Church supplicants, but their prayers are to the voodoo god. They want to know whether the loa is pleased with the ceremony.

The possessed person finally gives the word that the loa is pleased, and the family, hungan, and bush priest then leave the room. The devotee is left alone and, exhausted, will probably sleep through the night.

Occasionally, there is one more step in this ritual. If it has been discovered that the person has been possessed by an unfriendly loa, then that god must be prevented from doing harm to either the devotee or any member of her family. In such cases, after the baptism, a symbol for the god is put into some kind of receptacle and buried in the earth where it can do no damage.

These steps in the baptism of a loa will vary in detail from town to town and country to country. There is generally some kind of celebration which follows the baptism, a dance party, a supper, but this too varies from place to place.

The devotee's first loa becomes her mait-tete (master of the head). Whatever other gods possess her subsequently, and there probably will be many, the mait-tete will be the chief of all the gods for her, controlling whatever other gods come to "ride" her. It is also this first god who alone receives the baptismal rites, and the one loa which must be removed (another ritual) from her head when the devotee dies.

Not all worshipers of the voodoo gods experience possession, and no satisfactory reason has yet been given to explain why some are and some are not possessed. We do know that certain people are more susceptible to hypnosis than others, and that the rhythmic beat of the drum and the repetitious singing of a chant do possess the qualities of sound which make for hypnotism. But attempts to define possession as hypnosis fail. There are too many such possessions which occur without the drum beat and without the chanting.

The drums, the singing, the dancing at voodoo rituals undoubtedly excite the imagination and might readily lead to possession. But can this explain the possession of a spectator at the ceremonies who has not been singing or dancing?

Will hypnosis explain the sudden possession of a person who does not belong to a voodoo temple and who is an ardent practitioner of another faith? Will it explain the possession of skeptics who scoff at voodoo gods and beliefs? They too are abruptly taken with an unmistakable seizure by the voodoo loas.

The evidences of faith such as the miracles of the Old and the New Testament, the voices of Saint Michael, Saint Margaret and Saint Catherine which came to Joan of Arc, the stigmata—marks which resembled the wounds on Christ crucified—appearing on the body of Saint Francis, cannot be explained in the logic of nonbelievers, nor can they be argued. Possession by the voodoo loa is an experience that is fascinating, dramatic and, above all, mystical. As with all other religions, there is much in voodoo that is supernatural and simply has no mortal logic.

VOODOO DANCE

Havelock Ellis, the widely read English author, wrote, "to dance was at once to worship and to pray . . . to imitate the gods . . . to persuade them to work in the direction of our own desire."

Rumi, the religious Persian poet, wrote, "whosoever knows the power of the dance, dwells with God."

These quotations are especially true when applied to the voodoo dance. When dancing, the faithful worship the gods, and are with them. Among some of the non-conformist Christian sects which existed in old Russia, people danced and became possessed. While possessed, these Christians believed they were Jesus Christ, the Son of God. Voodoo dancers, while possessed, become a pantheon of gods.

Voodoo dancers dance to celebrate birth, death, and various stages in a person's life. They dance to thank the gods, or to ask their protection, or to pray for good fortune. They dance, too, in honor of some visiting celebrity, to conclude each sacred ritual, and to celebrate some national holiday. They dance, also, to honor the drums so essential to their dances.

Voodoo Drums

Drums have a special significance in the lives of the faithful.

There are sacred ceremonies which accompany the making of the drums. During voodoo rites it is not uncommon to see the hungan or the mambo, the hunsi, or one of the celebrants approach the drums, kneel before them, and sometimes kiss the ground on which they rest.

Before the tree from which the drum will be made is cut down, the hungan conducts a ceremony of adoration. When the trunk is hollowed out for the drum, the hungan pours rum into it and burns it in sacred ritual.

The finished drum will be in the shape of a cone, with two flattened ends. The sides of the drum will be painted in the colors of the principal god of the humfort to which the instrument will be attached. The head of the drum will be fashioned of goat skin or cow skin, stretched and tightened by wooden pegs. Driving the first hole for the first peg in the drum is celebrated with a special ritual.

For its baptism the drum is decorated, robed, and receives the full baptismal ceremonies accorded a person. There will be Catholic rites conducted by the bush priest and voodoo rites conducted by the hungan or mambo. The godparents for the drum will be present, and there will be sacrifices, feasting, and dancing.

A variety of drums are made for different loa to be worshiped in the voodoo dances. For the Rada gods there is the manman, which is about three-feet tall; the segond which measures about a foot and a half in height; and the bula which is from sixteen to twenty inches tall. All three drums are played at different pitches but their rhythms blend in their Rada dances.

The Petro dances require only two drums: the manman

and a smaller instrument, called the pititt or the ti-baka.

Congo dances utilize three instruments, the manman, the timebal, and the ti-congo. These drums are cylindrical and are made with two heads for the hands or the sticks of the drummer. Ibo drums are fashioned in a similar manner.

The djuba is a special, small, one-headed drum which is utilized in homage to Zaka, the peasant earth god.

The drums call the faithful to their dances. The drums summon the gods to the celebration. The drummer must know the special rhythms which will bring each loa as well as the beats which announce the dances. He must be familiar with the variety of voodoo dances. The beating of the drums, the rhythm and the tempo is the force which intensifies the religious ardor of the celebrants and brings the gods to possess them.

Saturday Night Dance

When the sun goes down on a Saturday night, the voodoo drums begin to sound through the twilight, and the faithful wend their way through the streets and alleys to join a celebration. Work in the fields is done, work in the plants is over. The government has granted permission for the ceremonies, and the devotees carry no obligation with them, except to allow the gods to use their bodies to dance.

There is some ritual to be observed, however, before the dancing may begin. The hungan takes a bottle of rum, pours some of it on the bonfire near the peristyle, in honor of the loa Legba. He takes a candle, approaches the drums which lie covered in some sort of cloth just at the entrance to the peristyle. He strikes each instrument once. He then splatters powder on the drums, and splashes some kind of alcoholic beverage on them. The drummers lift the drums over the entrance to the peristyle, and the hungan leads the drums on a ritual march—preceded by flag-waving hunsi—three times around the house of worship. The ceremony is sacred preparation for the instruments before they can take part in the celebration.

The dance itself starts slowly as the first celebrants arrive, but the pace quickens as their numbers grow. The instruments beat out their varying rhythms. The dancers move counter-clockwise around the poteau-mitan and the hunsi move freely among them shaking their rattles high over their heads. Occasionally worshipers will dance in pairs but generally each celebrant dances alone, and seems to be unaware of the other dancers.

There are different movements for the different gods. A heavy gait will denote homage to the earth god, Zaka. A martial step will indicate that the dancer has the war-god Ogun in mind. Undulating movements will indicate worship to Agwe, loa of the sea, or Damballa, the snake god. The loa Gede will inspire obscene, but nevertheless sacred, gestures. When possession takes over, it is the gods themselves—in the bodies of the celebrants—who are dancing.

The women will lift their skirts gently up and down as they dance. The men will gesticulate with their kerchiefs. Their movements will center primarily about their shoulders and their hips, rather than in the feet. When Gede is among them, he will gesture with his buttocks. Sometimes popular dance steps will find their way into the religious dancing, but usually in the form of improvisation, much as a jazz pianist will suddenly thrust a phrase from Chopin or Beethoven into his jazz composition. Voodoo dances have their own recognizable forms, but they allow for much invention on the part of the dancers.

A lantern is lit to give some light to the dancers. The

drummers place lighted candles on their drums. The hungan calls the loa down from the poteau-mitan to join their devotees.

The pace of the dancing becomes more lively. A celebrant is suddenly possessed by a loa. There will be many such possessions during the night. The possessed begins to stagger, reel, and to roll on the ground, and a hunsi is immediately dancing with her, to prevent any injury to the possessed.

The hunsi carries a shell of water and a lighted candle. His eyes are fixed on the eyes of the dancer, whom he slows down almost hypnotically. Slowly the celebrant comes out of her trance. The god begins to leave her. She begins to return to her senses.

She takes the shell of water and the lighted candle which the hunsi offers her. She moves, unsteadily, to the poteau-mitan. Here she pours some water from the shell and makes the sign of the cross with her candle, in homage to the poteau-mitan, and to the gods resting in it. She moves to the ogan and repeats the ritual. She goes through the rites once more, before each sacred drum. She is led into the house of worship or whatever other house has been made available for the purpose, where she may rest after her ordeal. If she has dirtied herself rolling in the mud, she may want to clean herself and change clothes.

Meanwhile, the dancing goes on to an ever quickening tempo. Damballa, Gede, Erzilie, and a host of other gods, possess their faithful, and each is calmed by a hunsi, or the hungan. By midnight there may be two hundred dancers and spectators at the ritual.

The passions and the fervor of the ceremony are infectious. Even the aged and the infirm, moved by the beat of the drums, suddenly find themselves possessed and lifted out of their chairs to dance around the poteau-mitan. When, with the aid of the hungan, these people are relieved of their loa, they return to their seats, exhausted, feeling older and even more infirm than before.

Even nonbelievers have been known to become possessed. People who are staunch Catholics or Protestants have been possessed by the voodoo gods. When the gods left them they had no memory of having danced.

Towards morning, the exhilarated but tired faithful begin the trek back to their homes. By sunrise there are just a few who have lingered behind. It is Sunday. Soon the ardent devotees of the voodoo loa are taking the Sabbath walk to church, to worship the God they believe is too far away to deal with their everyday problems.

In the cities, such as Port-au-Prince and Cap-Haitien, the voodoo dance has become a tourist attraction. The tendency in these cities is to make the voodoo celebration a spectacle rather than a ritual, and to over-dramatize something already highly dramatic. For a genuine voodoo dance, a person will have to leave the well-worn highways and find some hamlet where strangers are welcome.

Voodoo services and rituals are private affairs, open only to the hungan or mambo and their assistants, families and specially invited guests. The voodoo dance, except perhaps when it climaxes a family ceremony, is open to all. The whole town is made aware of the coming dance and is invited. At sunset, to the beat of the voodoo drums, the townspeople and their guests begin to walk to the celebration for the gods.

MAGIC—BOCORS, ZOMBIS, AND WEREWOLVES

According to anthropologists, magic has been in existence since the Stone Age. In Egypt, the magicians of Pharoah—according to the Bible—could duplicate the "magic" of the Hebrew God, turning a rod into a snake, a snake into a rod. There were powerful magicians among the ancient Greeks and the ancient Romans. The word "magic" comes from the word *Magi,* the name by which the priests of ancient Persia (modern Iran) were known.

Voodoo is not magic but there is much that is magic in voodoo. The gods of voodoo, like the gods in all religions, have the power to cause good fortune or bad. Witness the manner in which Job, of the Old Testament, was made to suffer because God wished to test his faith. These good or evil visitations of the gods on their flock are deemed supernatural because the gods themselves are supernatural. Magic, whatever its supernatural qualities, can only be defined as the work of man. As the people of voodoo say, it is the gods who grant the permission for the supernatural deed, but it is the magician who creates the many protective charms—"traitement," the "garde," the "arret" and the most powerful of protective charms, the "drogue." It is also the magician who manufactures the wanga, the evil charm which brings harm, illness, and even death.

Will the wearing of a copper bracelet, a common practice today, arrest the development of arthritis and ease its pain? Is the bracelet a sound medical remedy, a piece of jewelry or is it a magic charm to ward off sickness? In the voodoo world the faithful do not ask such questions. They do not doubt the power of the magic charm.

In voodoo belief, minor misfortune can usually be cured by offering the family loa an extra candle, food, or some other small token to let the loa know that they are not being neglected. A minor illness may very well be a sign, to a voodoo family, that the loa are not particularly happy with the homage they are receiving. But, should the sickness be of a serious nature, the family will hasten to get advice and help from its hungan or mambo.

It is the hungan who will divine—perhaps through his cards, perhaps in a seance with the loa—the cause of the misfortune and suggest a remedy. Sometimes the prescription for getting rid of misfortune will require little more than the gathering and use of certain roots and herbs. The hungan generally has a thorough knowledge of the curative powers of herbs and roots, and his prescription often will result in a cure.

This treatment, however, is certainly ineffective against financial misfortune and death. At such times the hungan is likely to advise a more intense service to the loa. The greater show of devotion could be a service in the house of worship, a dance to honor Legba or any of the other gods who may have been offended.

Bocor—the Evil Magician

When calamity is persistent—a series of unexpected

deaths in the family, or a quick series of business misadventures—there is no doubt that the family may be suffering because of an evil charm. The hungan, by way of his cards or a seance, will determine if there is a curse, where it is located, and how it might be destroyed.

Except for perhaps in the simple remedies using roots and herbs, the hungan is never without concern for the desires of the loa. Even in the manufacture of a charm to stop evil or to cause good the loa is consulted. The charm may be nothing more than a small sack of leaves, powders, shells, and the like, but it is created according to the order of the gods, blessed by a Church prayer, and made sacred by a phrase or two of voodoo magic. The hungan makes the charm, but it is the loa who grants permission for its making and its use.

The evil magician is no less concerned with the loa. It is the voodoo gods who permit him to fashion his wanga. The gods allow him to tamper with the corpses of the dead and fetch them out of their graves for evil purposes.

Mait Carrefour, Saint Expedit, Baron Samedi, and Gede are the principal deities in the voodoo pantheon for the bocor. These are the gods who define and sometimes limit his powers. Saint Expedit properly belongs to the Church, but the bocor deals primarily with the image of the saint, a statue. The bocor consults with Mait Carrefour, sometimes called Legba-petro, at the crossroads where the god lives. He finds Baron Samedi and Gede behind the crosses in the cemeteries.

For the most powerful of his evil spells, those which can kill, the bocor invokes first the good will and the aid of Saint Expedit. Saint Expedit is the god who can "send the dead" to enter the body of the living, where the "dead" may slowly, or quickly, kill its host.

For this "expedition," as the "sending of the dead" is

called, the bocor follows a prescribed ritual. Together with his "client," under the cover of the darkness of the night, the evil magician finds a convenient crossroad, or goes directly to some cemetery. There he turns the image of Saint Expedit—which he brings with him—upside down, places it on the ground, and begins his rites.

First, he calls on God, the Father, to find the intended victim and to wipe him or her off the face of the earth. This is the "Catholic" part of the ceremony. The Church is never neglected, even by the evil magician.

Next, the practical bocor calls on Saint Expedit to be his patron saint. He names the intended victim and asks the saint to destroy every trace of him, including his memory. Not at all modest in his requests, the bocor asks that his own enemies, living and dead, be destroyed with thunder and lightning. The bocor ends this un-churchly plea with Paternosters for the saint. The Church elements of the ritual completed, the magician begins the voodoo rites.

Baron Samedi is invoked. The god possesses the bocor, and speaks to the client—the person who has requested the expedition. The god tells the client precisely what food and beverage he must bring to him as an offering. The offering is usually made at midnight, and it is left behind the cross where the deity lives. Next, Baron Samedi tells the client to pick up a handful of dirt for each "dead" to be sent against the intended victim. The client may also be instructed to pick up a number of stones lying around a grave-site. The dirt will be spread along the paths most frequented by the intended victim, so that he will step on it and thus permit the dead to enter his body. The stones are to be tossed against the house of the intended victim so that the dead might enter through its door.

A voodoo charm for protection against sorcerers

These rituals performed, both the bocor and the client are certain that the dead will find and enter the victim's body, and destroy him. And strangely enough, unless the loa Gede refuses to dig the grave, or unless certain strenuous voodoo rituals are performed as an antidote, the victim will die.

If Gede, the loa of justice in such cases, does not think the victim's death is warranted, there will be no killing. This does not mean the victim's troubles are over. The victim will become seriously ill and suffer great agony.

The antidote for this killing wanga, if discovered in time, involves the performance of an elaborate voodoo ritual. It is a ritual which closely resembles the rites given to someone deceased, and concludes with ceremonies which resemble an enactment of resurrection.

The intended victim is laid out like a corpse. The nose and ears are almost completely stuffed with cotton wool. The mouth is kept closed by means of a cord strapped to the top of the head. The big toes are tied together. There are the Church prayers for the dead, Church chants, voodoo prayers and chants. There is the ritual bathing with scented water, the rubbing with leaves and oil. There are the offerings of sacrificed chickens, pigeons, and sometimes a goat. At some point during the ceremony, the hungan will offer "to buy" the victim from the gods. Strangely enough, by magic or faith, the person who has been very sick, will slowly, then quickly, become strong and healthy.

Bocors have other ways for dealing death to the faithful. They know how to "arrange" some piece of cloth, a stone, a kitchen utensil, a chicken, almost anything, in such a manner that it will bring sickness or death to whoever touches it.

The sticking of pins, or the hammering of nails, into a doll, an image, or likeness, is another of the bocor's death-dealing devices. This sort of pin-sticking practice, of course, is not peculiar to voodoo. Thousands of years ago, similar killing rituals were used in Egypt, Greece, Rome,

China, and Africa. In Japan the manikin was buried upside down under a rotting tree for the same purpose.

Zombi—Raising the Dead

The practice of raising the dead for evil purpose is unique to the black magic of the bocor. By magic known only to the bocor, the corpse is lifted from its grave to become a zombi—the evil doer's docile servant.

In voodoo belief the zombi moves in a completely lethargic manner. It can hear, possibly talk, but is completely without memory until its mouth touches salt. The taste of salt will suddenly bring the zombi to its senses, and it will hurry back to the cemetery to return to its grave.

Zombis are completely under the bocor's control. They are made to work like beasts of burden. They are even forced to steal, and commit other crimes. The bocor may have several zombis working in his household and he may even sell them from time to time.

There is no antidote in voodoo for being turned into a zombi. But the faithful, aware of the bocor's magic, will take steps to avoid this happening to one of their own. Commonly, people inject poison into the body of someone whose death is believed to be unnatural. Because of the voodoo belief that a corpse must answer to its name before it can be raised from its grave, the lips of the dead may be sewn together, so that they cannot speak. Needles with broken eyes are buried with the dead so that they can spend eternity in a futile attempt to thread them. Countless numbers of seeds are placed in the coffin to keep the dead occupied forever trying to count them.

Despite all these precautions, according to story and legend, the zombi is said to be found almost anywhere. He may be recognized by the empty stare in his eyes, the listlessness of his gait, and the lifelessness of his arms and legs.

There are drugs which have the power to create a lethargy similar to the lethargy of the zombi. This might lead us to conclude that the bocor utilizes such drugs. Whatever the case, the Haitian authorities have decreed that anyone who creates a state of lethargy in another may be charged with the intention to kill. Should this state of lethargy result in death, then the guilty person may be charged with murder. In a not too subtle fashion, the authorities recognize the possible, if not the actual, existence of the zombi.

In the world of voodoo the practitioner of black magic is understandably much feared. Certainly his clients do not employ him without trepidation. But the bocor does not go about his business entirely without fear, either. For all his mischief, mayhem and perhaps murder, the bocor is always concerned with the possibility of offending the loa. The angry loa may punish the magician as easily as they punish anyone else.

The clients of the bocors must concern themselves with the loa's possible disapproval of their dealings with the evil magicians. They must also worry about reprisals from their intended victims. The victims might as readily employ bocors on their own, to avenge the evils visited on them.

Werewolf

But bocors do not constitute the only cause for fear in the voodoo scene. There are, for example, the werewolves, and the vampires, usually female, that kill by sucking the blood out of the veins of their victims.

The werewolf, of course, has appeared throughout history almost everywhere. It is a human being, maybe the good next-door neighbor, until it sheds its skin to become the murdering animal. There are, according to legend, certain ways to recognize a werewolf when it appears in its "human" state. In Denmark, it was said that the telltale marks were its eyebrows: if they met, they were the eyebrows of a werewolf. In the voodoo world, it is the red eyes, or a black spot in the eyes of a human, which disclose the presence of a werewolf. So powerful was the belief in the existence of this horrible creature that, in the fifteenth century, a council of eminent theologians, meeting in Hungary, declared that werewolves were real, not imaginary creatures.

Werewolves among the voodoo people seem to have a preference for the blood of children. According to magic formula, the werewolf must procure the mother's permission before it may attack the child. This permission is generally obtained when the mother is preoccupied with doing something else and not quite aware of what she is saying. Permission is also gained when the mother is half-asleep. Werewolves, according to the legend, can change their skins and forms into the shape of any animal they wish. They can become large or small. To find their prey, they generally get into a house as tiny insects, unseen and unheard.

Voodoo mothers of course will do all in their power to keep their children secure from the designs of the werewolf. They will wear every kind of talisman the hungan or mambo advises. When they are pregnant, they will drink a concoction of coffee, rum and gasoline which is supposed to make the blood of the infant distasteful to the werewolf. They will take all kinds of special baths, designed by the hungan, to keep the werewolf away from their children. They will feed their offspring unpleasant foods to create bad blood which will drive the werewolf out of their children's beds. The bad blood might even kill the beast.

The werewolf is not the last of those to be feared in the voodoo world. There are magicians and sorcerers, other than the bocors, who have sold their souls to the evil spirits. They, too, have the power to change their sizes and shapes. They are the ones who become the wild and horrendous-looking beasts that innocent travelers meet on lonely roads and in the darkness. These creatures, too, are found in the fairy tales of every land. Nevertheless, story or legend, there are roaming bands of men who call themselves by such names as the "Hairless Pigs," "Grey Pigs," "Hairless Ones." To meet with them alone is to invite disaster. These bands of "zobops," as they are called in Haiti, are also known as the "red sects." They have been accused of willful murder. They have also been accused of cannibalism.

It would seem that there is enough in voodoo lore to keep the faithful close to home after dark. But the drums begin to beat with the setting of the sun and the faithful go forth to dance and to worship their loa.

10

VOODOO AND THE CHURCH

The Christian Church has converted millions of people on every continent of the world. Over the centuries, the "heathen" and the "pagan" have been turned away from ancient beliefs in ancient gods and taught to worship the Father, the Son and the Holy Ghost. In most places the Church was successful. Native peoples gave up their old gods and took on new ones.

In Haiti the great majority of African slaves became Christian, but they developed a curiously compatible relationship between this and their continued worship of African gods. The voodoo faithful insist that their children be baptized in the Catholic faith. They send their children to church for their first communion. They make their confessions regularly in church (often on the advice of their hungan or mambo). They get married in church. They attend mass. And they will receive extreme unction from a priest of the Church, whenever possible, or from a bush priest as a last resort.

The voodoo faithful equate membership in the Church with prestige. It is the kind of prestige which the first slaves attached to the ritual of baptism. It is the kind of prestige similar to that which some people get by becoming members of a country club, or the Elks, the Lions, the Rotarians.

The rituals of the Church, too, as we have already seen, can be incorporated into voodoo ceremony and pressed into service for the voodoo gods. The action de grace (prayer of thanksgiving), the Paternoster, Ave Maria, Credo precede the voodoo rites at every voodoo celebration. The holy water of the Church, despite the watchful eye of its priests, is regularly used in the voodoo rites of baptism. The hunsi kanzo are baptized with holy water. So too are the voodoo drums, rattles, necklaces, and even their loa, in Church ceremony when possible, in the humfort if necessary. According to reports, the Host has been stolen from the Church time and time again, principally by the bocors for the practice of their evil magic.

We have read how the voodoo faithful identify the saints of the Church with their gods. Similarly, the crucifix, the rosaries, and other Church images have become symbols of voodoo worship.

For all this voodoo adaptation of Church symbol and practice, however, the voodoo faithful still consider themselves good Catholics. One cannot be a worshiper of voodoo without being a good Catholic, they say. They will go to church, when the church bells summon them, though they will tell you that the bells are ringing for Legba, so that he may open the gates for all the other gods, including the Father, the Son and the Holy Ghost. They will march in Church parades, take part in Church festivals, and celebrate the Church holy days, though they will do all this with something of a voodoo touch. And they will always be certain, in accordance with their faith, to call on a bush priest to lend the aura of the Church to their voodoo rites.

The Church, for its part, frowns on all these voodoo

practices. It views all voodoo rituals as exercises in superstition, at best—as the work of the devil, at worst. According to the catechism of the Church, as it is taught in Haiti, the hungan and mambo are the slaves of Satan. The loa, the dead, and the marassa, the catechism teaches, are names the hungan and mambo give to Satan. The Church says Satan is served by the practice of magic, by the offerings made to the loa, by the casting of spells. The Protestant churches of Haiti also sternly view voodoo as an abomination.

Late in the 1890s the Catholic Church launched a concerted attack on the practices of voodoo in Haiti. A League Against Voodoo was organized under the auspices of the bishop of Cap-Haitien. The league consisted of parishioners and priests. It campaigned against the "superstitions" of voodoo, but had little or no support from the civilian government. The president of Haiti declared himself in favor of the campaign but the majority of people in high government posts, born and bred in the atmosphere of voodoo, were not inclined to challenge the loa, however little they personally believed in or worshiped them. Despite the bishop's threat of religious sanctions against those who continued in their voodoo ways, the anti-voodoo campaign finally had to be abandoned.

There were other sporadic efforts on the part of the Church and each effort met defeat. Not until 1939 did the Church mount an attack which cut seriously into the numbers of the voodoo faithful, but not without creating a situation approaching chaos.

With government approval and the help of the army, priests and laymen raided the houses of worship and the homes of people suspected of voodoo practice. They seized every object which might in any way relate to voodoo —rattles, govi, drums, beads. They built huge bonfires and burned everything including colored lithographs of the saints. The same pictures posted in the churches did not go into the flames.

Thousands of Haitians, under the threat of being denied Church sacraments, swore to stop worshiping the loa. Thousands of others, swept up by the fervor of the crusade, voluntarily appeared in the churches to renounce their voodoo beliefs forever.

The anti-voodoo campaign might have succeeded in banishing the loa for all time, but the Church, in its overconfidence, made a serious mistake. The Church decided that all Haitians be required to swear an oath of affirmation and rejection. The "rejector," as the one taking the oath was called, was to swear never again to attend any kind of voodoo ceremony, or practice any voodoo rites. Then the rejector had to affirm that every voodoo object in his possession had been destroyed. Finally the person was to pledge to remain true to the Catholic faith as long as he lived and bring up his children in the faith as well.

Those people who had never been involved in voodoo practice resented the request for the oath. They looked on it as a humiliating affront. The many thousands more who had concealed their voodoo worship were perhaps louder in their opposition to the oath, and with good reason. In either case, despite the arguments and the propaganda of the Church, less than one percent of Haiti's church population took the all-embracing vow.

Initially there was practically no resistance to the raids on the voodoo sacred places and the homes of voodoo worshipers. The presence of the army made sure of that. But resistance to the required oath, the newspapers' criticism of the overzealous actions of the clergy, and the relaxation of support on the part of the government's army brought about a gradual but dramatic change.

The voodoo faithful, coming out of hiding, began to express profound resentment of the Church's crusade against their faith. There were sporadic "religious strikes," something in the nature of mass demonstrations. Finally, during a mass in a church near Port-au-Prince, on 22 February 1942, shots were fired and a near panic followed. The government decided to curb the Church's campaign against voodoo.

There were some who said that the shooting was arranged by the government, that soldiers dressed as peasants had fired the shots. Whatever the truth, certainly the government had become increasingly concerned with possible excesses in the Church's crusade. There were probably any number of people, high in the government ranks, who feared they might be exposed as voodooist by the Church's probing. In any event, the reaction in Haiti to the government's action was one of relief and joy. There was a quick and open return to voodoo practice.

Beginning with the French occupation and colonization, Haiti has been and still is a Catholic country, but there has been some growth among the Protestant sects. When people wish completely to cut their ties with voodoo they join a Protestant church. According to one knowledgeable Haitian, the converts stay in the Protestant church until they have difficulties. As soon as they cannot resolve their problems, they return to voodoo.

11

RELIGION OR SUPERSTITION

Are superstition and magic the ingredients of voodoo, as is so often charged? Or is it a religion, like Catholicism, Protestantism or any of the other many faiths of the world?

According to the theological definition of most established religions, faith is the unquestioning acknowledgment of the power of a supreme being. The voodoo faithful, as we have read, worship the Father, the Son and the Holy Ghost and have no doubts concerning their supreme powers.

Faith, according to most theologians, calls for the acceptance of a divine order as a reality. There is nothing more real to the voodoo faithful than the divine order. It differs from the orders of other religions in that it includes not only saints, but the dead and the marassa.

The Catholic clergy of Haiti, in its "anti-superstition" campaign, burned the voodoo drums, rattles and other instruments because they considered these objects fetishes of the devil. This was not the first time in history that the members of one faith destroyed the sacred objects of another's faith. And it is always the "righteous" who, in the service of God, destroy the works of one kind of Satan or another. Who is to say that, in the eyes of the Almighty, the symbols of one faith are sacred and others are abominations? Is the crucifix less sacred because it lies on a voodoo altar? Are the pictures of the saints less sacred because they adorn a voodoo wall? Who shall say that the worship of the Almighty in the voodooist's humfort is less sacred than the worship of God in a temple, in a church, or in a cathedral?

Voodoo ritual, too, has been a constant target for abuse. Even people kindly disposed to voodoo have labeled its ceremonies as so much hocus-pocus. Perhaps it has never occurred to them that in the eyes of voodoo adherents the rituals of other faiths may seem less than blessed.

The history of the Church is replete with schisms caused by disputes over ritual. The separation of the Protestants from Rome was based, to a considerable degree, on such a dispute. The Protestant Church itself is divided into a great number of sects, primarily because of ritual differences. Yet, are the Quakers less Christian for their form of worship than are the Shakers, or the Baptists or the Methodists or the Episcopalians?

Obviously the nature of a congregation's rituals is no measure of its faith. The magnificent mass of the Catholic Church, the simple prayers of a Protestant sect, the enthusiastic singing, shouting, hand-clapping in a Spiritualist church, the invocation of the gods in voodoo, all give evidence of devotion. Faith and devotion are phenomena possessed only by men and women, and their children. They constitute an eternal link between humans and their God or gods.

Magic is perhaps the most misinterpreted of all elements in the voodoo world. As has been said before, many times, there is magic in voodoo, but voodoo is not magic. Actually there is magic in all faiths.

If a parent prays for the recovery of a sick child and the child gets well, we say that the Lord has heard the prayers. Airplane pilots come home "on a wing and a prayer," a prayer which has been answered by the Lord. We do not call these happy responses to our supplications magic, but we do believe that the Almighty, with his supernatural powers, has intervened in our behalf.

Let us recall that all voodoo magicians, even the evil bocor, request permission from their gods before they may create a charm, an amulet, for good or for evil. Shall we call this an exercise in magic? Saint Expedit (of the Church) is invoked to send "the dead," and the voodoo faithful believe he does. Is this magic? There is an old saw which goes, "One man's meat is another man's poison." Is it possible that one man's magic may be another man's faith? and vice-versa?

We have explored the area of superstition before. Let us add a few other superstitions which still prevail among us. We still knock on wood to avert misfortune. We still say, "God bless you," when someone sneezes. On opening night at the theater, actors send their actor friends telegrams which read, "Break a leg," because they think such messages will bring good luck. Bridegrooms are not supposed to see their brides in bridal dress before the wedding ceremony, lest some evil befall their union. Certainly voodoo, too, has many of its own superstitions, but does that make voodoo itself superstition?

Voodoo has taboos, too. So does every other faith. The Ten Commandments, delivered by the Lord to Moses on Mount Sinai, carry nine restrictions in behavior for the true believers. Leviticus and Deuteronomy, in the Holy Bible, are replete with commands which might readily be interpreted as taboos. Obviously, taboos may be of a profoundly religious nature. Voodoo taboos may seem less profound to us. Does this reduce their religious significance? Does this make the religion less a sacred faith?

It was the Chinese philosopher, Lao-tse, who said, centuries ago that many paths lead to God. Perhaps we can conclude by suggesting that voodoo follows one of those paths.

BIBLIOGRAPHY

Arciniegas, Germán. *Latin America: A Cultural History.* New York: Knopf, 1967,

Bach, Marcus. *Strange Altars.* New York: Bobbs-Merrill, 1952.

Bascom, William R. "The Focus on Santeria." Albuquerque, N. Mex. *Southwestern Journal of Anthropology,* 1950.

Bohannan, Paul. *Africa and Africans.* New York: Natural History Press, 1964.

Courlander, Harold. "Musical Instruments of Haiti." New York. *The Musical Quarterly,* vol. 37, no. 3, July 1941, pp. 171–83.

Craige, John H. *Black Bagdad.* New York: Minton, Balch, 1933.

Deren, Maya. *Divine Horsemen.* New York: Chelsea House, 1970.

Frazer, Sir James G. *The Golden Bough.* New York: Criterion, 1947.

Grimal, Pierre. *Larousse World Mythology.* New York: Prometheus, 1965.

Herring, Hubert. *A History of Latin America.* New York: Knopf, 1968.

Herskovits, Melville, J. *Life in a Haitian Valley.* New York: Knopf, 1937.

Horowitz, M. M. *Peoples and Cultures of the Caribbean.* New York: Natural History Press, 1971.

Houston, Zora. *Voodoo Gods.* London: Dent, 1939.

Leyburn, James G. *The Haitian People.* New Haven: Yale Press, 1945.

Loederer, Richard A. *Voodoo Fire in Haiti.* New York: Doubleday, 1936.

Metraux, Alfred. *Voodoo in Haiti.* New York: Schocken, 1972.

Pearcy, G. Etzel. *The West Indian Scene.* Princeton: Von Nostrand, 1965.

Rigaud, Milo. *Secrets of Voodoo.* New York: Arco, 1970.

Seabrook, W. B. *The Magic Island.* New York: Literary Guild, 1929.

Simpson, George E. "Four Vodun Ceremonies." *Philadelphia Journal of American Folklore,* vol. 59, no. 231, 1946, pp. 154–67.

———. "The Belief System of Haitian Vodun." Menasha, Wisc. *American Anthropologist,* vol. 47, no. 1, 1945, pp. 35–59.

Tallant, Robert. *Voodoo in New Orleans.* New York: Macmillan, 1946.

William, Joseph J. *Voodoos and Obeahs.* London: Allen, 1932.

INDEX

ABOUT THE AUTHOR

Henry Gilfond is the author of numerous young adult books, including *Black Hand at Sarajevo,* and *The Reichstag Fire* (A World Focus Book), published by Franklin Watts. He has written for radio, television, and the theater, edited literary and dance magazines, and done reviews for the *New York Times Book Review.* He lives in New York City with his wife, Edythe, a costume designer.